OOBLECK, SLIME + DANCING SPAGHETTI

bright sky press

2365 Rice Blvd., Suite 202 Houston, Texas 77005

10   9   8   7   6   5   4   3   2   1

Library of Congress Cataloging-in-Publication Data

Williams, Jennifer, 1971-

Oobleck, slime, and dancing spaghetti : 20 terrific at-home science experiments inspired by favorite children's books / by Jennifer Williams.

p. cm.

Includes bibliographical references.

ISBN 978-1-933979-34-2 (pbk. : alk. paper)

1. Science--Experiments—Juvenile literature. I. Title.

Q164.W538 2008

507.8—dc22   2009000876

Book and cover design by Cregan Design

Cover (illustrated portion) by Elaine Atkinson

Edited by Shelley Pannill Stein and Nora Shire

Printed in China through Asia Pacific Offset

OOBLECK, SLIME + DANCING SPAGHETTI

Twenty Terrific

At-Home Science

Experiments

Inspired by

Favorite

Children's Books

Jennifer Williams

Recipient of the Presidential Award
for Excellence in Mathematics and Science Teaching

 bright sky press
HOUSTON, TEXAS

To M.E.H.

My first critic and my biggest supporter.

Thank you, and all my love.

"The whole art of teaching is only the art of awakening the natural curiosity of young minds for the purpose of satisfying it afterwards."

– Anatole France, 19th century French poet and novelist

Table of Contents

Part 3: Air Science and Engineering

Part 4: Meteorology

INTRODUCTION

Many of my fondest childhood memories of science involve sitting with my father, an electrical engineer, at the kitchen table tinkering with his model train collection. We would watch, listen, and put circuits together to make the cars move from station to station and back. We would spend hours building engines and generators that made smoke appear or caused the locomotive's whistle to sound.

In fifth grade, my class studied a unit on circuits. While many of my classmates struggled, I was so knowledgeable about the structure and functioning of circuits that my teacher allowed me to diagram them on the board. I felt both proud of my easy grasp of open and closed circuitry and elated at sharing my knowledge with my classmates.

Even so, science in school never quite lived up to science with Dad. I recall memorizing the Periodic Table of the Elements, balancing chemical formulas, creating dichotomous keys for identifying plant and animal species, and memorizing the scientific name for those living beings. These scientific concepts had little relevance to my life or to my dad's train set. I could not see much of a connection to what I was learning in other subject areas or to my future aspirations.

As I advanced, science class became more abstract and less real. It came easy for me, but I could not picture myself as the stereotypical scientist in the white lab coat with thick glasses and a pocket protector.

So how did I end up a science teacher?

Fast-forward a few years. I was working as an elementary school teacher in a Louisiana public school. I taught social studies, reading, and drama, but not science. And I realized that I missed it! I could always see the connection science had to events in history: the Industrial Revolution, the development of weaponry during the Civil War and World War I. In drama class, I would make a scientific lesson out of creating special effects, lighting, and sound.

After four years of integrating science into these classes, I gladly became a science teacher at Isidore Newman, a rigorous and prestigious independent school in New Orleans. My

11

challenge: How to teach basic chemistry to third-graders? While astronomy and botany were relatively easy sells, I didn't want to bog down or frustrate my 8-year-olds with the Periodic Table.

Then, an epiphany: Cooking is chemistry!

Chemistry, of course, is the science of how materials combine and react under different conditions. I remember "feeding yeast" in my grandmother's kitchen in preparation for bread-making. I loved mixing ingredients together and watching cakes rise through the oven window. My grandmother was teaching me the basics of chemistry — just as my father had taught me about circuitry!

A word about incorporating food into the lessons: Children love to eat. Some can never get enough. As they watch and help prepare food, children are not only using their senses to understand what is happening, but they are also developing their scientific processing skills: questioning, observing, analyzing, and synthesizing.

To make the kitchen chemistry even more accessible, I decided to go "cross-curricular" again. I brought in beloved storybooks that would feed the kids' imaginations and inspire even more creativity. When I introduced an experiment with a story, I found that my students had improved associations with the concepts we "cooked up" in the lab.

That is how I designed what has become the central feature of my curriculum and the focus of this book: Mixing science, cooking, and children's literature into a unit of study. Over the past ten years, I have taken the idea to other scientific realms: Physics, botany, environmental science, geology, and entomology.

The combination really works: Students are able to identify with the characters and see science "unfold" in settings similar to their own lives — or, in some cases, in wildly imaginative, wonderful settings. And children are much more excited about picture books and fictional tales than they are about textbooks, which are often dry and unappealing. Finally, the science presented in children's books is so cleverly introduced that most children do not recognize they are learning science unless it is pointed out...kind of like how I learned circuitry with Dad.

This book is intended to guide parents who want to instill their children with the same wonder and excitement I first encountered at the kitchen table. The most important ingredient is already there in the form of your child's innate curiosity. You can do all of the experiments, "recipes," and activities using ordinary kitchen tools. Some experiments can be done using metric measuring cups and spoons, which can be found in a drug store or hospital pharmacy.

The step-by-step explanations and ingredient lists make these experiments as easy to put together as a batch of cookies. And sprinkled throughout the text are little reminders about scientific principles for those parents who, like me, were initially frustrated or bored by the Periodic Table.

In the end, I hope the book will inspire both you and your child to explore the world with excitement and imagination and develop a lifelong passion for learning how things work. If one of you should fall in love with chemistry or — why not? — electrical engineering, all the better!

WHY SCIENCE?

Science is the process of acquiring knowledge through exploration and experimentation in order to understand the natural world. Simply put, science class is the time of day when experiments are meant to fail or surprise us, when mistakes are expected and learned from, and when the order of the day is to discover what makes the things around us tick.

Why now?

Multiple studies suggest that the time allocated for science instruction at the elementary level in the United States has significantly decreased since the enactment of the No Child Left Behind (NCLB) Act in 2002. Because school performance scores — not to mention state and federal funding — are based on the math and English language arts portions of high-stakes testing, these classes have become the main focus of our elementary schools. Instruction time for subjects like science, social studies, and the arts has significantly decreased in some states.

At the same time, test scores show that U.S. students lag behind their international counterparts in science. What this means is that science literacy in the United States continues to decline. This can and will put a strain on the economy. Science is a part of every major U.S. industry: Medicine, transportation, military defense, farming, manufacturing, food preparation, and natural resource management, to name a few.

A broader goal should be for everyone — age and nationality notwithstanding — to have a basic level of scientific knowledge, argue the authors of Benchmarks for Scientific Literacy: "People who are literate in science... are able to use the habits of mind and knowledge of science, mathematics, and technology they have acquired to think about and make sense of many of the ideas, claims, and events that they encounter in everyday life."

If we think of science as the school subject of discovery and experimentation, then children in the post-NCLB era risk missing out on some crucial learning opportunities in school.

Why me?

Or: Do I have to be a microbiologist or a chemist to teach my kid about science?

You do not — repeat do not — have to be a scientist to teach your child about science. Just like my Dad, you are your child's first teacher. Not only does your child absorb your words like a sponge, she also soaks up your attitudes. Your enthusiasm for learning and experimentation as well as the topics you expose her to will influence your child's future learning. After all, it was my Dad's excitement that got me started on circuitry, not simply the subject matter.

And as I will remind you over and again, children are "science-ready" at birth. "Young children are natural mathematicians and scientists," say experts at the National Science Foundation, because of their endless curiosity, their desire to explore, and their natural ability to take risks. By fostering that curiosity, you will provide her with valuable concepts, life skills, and, eventually, career options — not to mention a great vocabulary! Science helps give kids a greater appreciation for the world and its inhabitants, a healthy dose of skepticism, strong problem-solving skills, and research know-how.

15

How do I do it?

First, shoppers beware: There is no need to run to your local toy store to purchase pricey experiment kits for your child. There is no need to go online to science supply stores to buy hundreds of dollars' worth of equipment and chemicals. Instead, begin with a basic tool of childhood — a story!

Many parents are already sold on the idea of reading to their kids. (And if you're not convinced yet, consider checking out *The Read-Aloud Handbook* by Jim Trelease.) On one level, stories and books are a great "entertainment" option for our kids as we read and cuddle with them. They give us snuggle and bonding time and help both parent and child unwind at bedtime. Good children's literature can pave the way for important conversations and questions between parent and child.

Of course, books also help children develop cognitively and linguistically. The more a child learns to enjoy children's literature, the more likely he is to learn from it, retain its information, and want to keep reading in the future.

Integrating science skills and ideas takes story time to the next level. Research shows that children benefit from the integration of science and literacy skills because they build associations between prior knowledge or skills (if they know how to read) and new material — in this case, scientific concepts. Kids can also see how science fits into the lives of people like them (or beloved non-human characters) in familiar (or fantastical) settings. As a result, science is no longer simply an isolated subject taught only in a lab. It is no longer a "hard" subject or boring. Science — like Strega Nona's magical noodles and Larry's ice cream — becomes a natural part of your child's life and imagination.

BEFORE YOU BEGIN:

How to use this book

These tips will help you guide your budding scientist through the experiments in this book.

- **A note regarding gender:** I will alternate references to "your child" as either "him" or "her" to make the text read more smoothly. You should not assume that any of these experiments would be better suited for a boy or a girl. Boys and girls are equally good at science. Remember, science is for everyone.

- **Your child is already a scientist.** She was born that way: Curious about her surroundings and prone to daily experimentation as she learned to build with blocks, lace her shoes, and make mountains out of her mashed potatoes. As such, it is important to bring her into the experiments in this book by giving her "ownership" of the procedures. The best approach is allowing him to handle as many of the tasks as possible, or if two children are doing it together, have them take turns. You may choose to read the instructions aloud to your child or children.

- **Never criticize your child's technique.** Explain clearly and gently what is important before he does it: "Pour slowly so it doesn't overflow," for instance. Practice steps like pouring and measuring amounts before starting the experiment. The more practice your child has with these tasks, the more successful he will feel when the experiment is successful.

- **Be safe! Work together!** These science "recipes" require adult supervision. Make sure you, the adult, handle any potentially caustic chemicals like Borax. Remind your child of the importance of washing his or her hands before making anything edible, like butter or ice cream. Practice "science safety" when working with chemicals and projectiles by wearing eye protection like goggles.

- **Keep a pencil handy.** We've provided sample data sheets you can photocopy and give to your child to note his or her results, as instructed. For some experiments that don't

17

require data sheets, we provide a blank sheet of a "scientist's notebook." Your child can doodle, brainstorm, draw, and even render scientific results using crayons! You might want to explain that in a lab, when scientists "gather data," it just means they write down details about what they have noticed along the way, such as reaction time, color, differences in the result based on time and temperature, and so forth. Gathering information in this way helps scientists to find patterns and make discoveries.

- **Quantitative vs. qualitative.** You may also want to explain to your child that there are two different types of data: Quantitative and qualitative. Qualitative data is subjective and has non-measurable details such as color, texture, and/or taste. Quantitative data is measurable information such as temperature, reaction time, changes in weight, or distance traveled.

- **Adding it all up.** All the measuring, observation, data collection and analysis your child will do while learning about the scientific process also makes for some great practice at math skills. Think about it this way: Science and math are integrated in the real science lab. They are not used in isolation. The same is true here. So not only will you be reading, experimenting and learning new science concepts with your child, you'll also be using real-life activities to reinforce her ease with the fundamentals of math!

- **Repeat, Repeat, Repeat.** While you may feel that these experiments are completed in one "take," remember that scientists in a lab setting repeat experiments, looking for consistency in data and results. Or they change one factor, referred to in science as a variable, to see how it will affect their results. Therefore, I encourage you and your child to conduct these experiments more than once. Not only will you reinforce the idea behind the experiment, but also your child will continue to hone his observation, fine motor, and math skills.

- **Age appropriateness:** The "recommended age" icons (see Key, p. 20) should help you determine if the experiment in question is appropriate for your child. However, don't rule out any of these experiments based on my age suggestions.

To make an experiment more little-kid friendly, simply do more yourself and have your child do less. Instead of having your four-year-old or kindergartener fill in the data sheet, you can fill it in. Or have them use crayons to express things like colors or minutes. To make a simple experiment more interesting for your older child, simply present them with more of the science and have her do the data recording, pouring, and so forth.

- **Hints as you go:** I have already encouraged you to allow your child to participate as much as possible in the experiments. Only take the reins when you see [parent icon]. At the same time, you must be in charge of the experiment. In order to give parents a full understanding of the experiment and what to expect, I will include helpful hints along the way.

  When you see this icon, try not to let curious eyes peek. We want to keep these "hints" hidden from them so they can discover the results on their own. This is the idea of pure and guided inquiry that is so stressed by the National Academies of Science.

- **Books.** The selections of children's literature accompanying and inspiring these experiments are tried-and-true vehicles for them. Most should be available at your public library, and all are available through Amazon.com. In some cases, we will suggest similar books you can use if you can't locate our suggestion or if you want a simpler or more complex book. In a pinch, you can do most of these experiments without even using the book, just based on our summary, but I recommend finding the book if you can!

- **No crying over spilled ... oobleck?** Like many childhood pursuits, science is messy. You should expect your child to spill or provoke a reaction that oozes or fizzes. Some of the parents I have worked with over the years were horrified at the idea that their children get messy and dirty while doing science. If you are worried about the mess, make sure to conduct the experiments in a "mess zone" and to have an apron for yourself and your children.

AGES: ICONS

PRE-K AND UP

K AND UP

2ND GRADE AND UP

4TH GRADE AND UP

HELPFUL HINTS

PARENT SUPERVISION

"DANGER"

for steps in experiments that are
risky or involve hot surfaces

SAFETY

PART I

Chemistry and Polymers

NOTES:

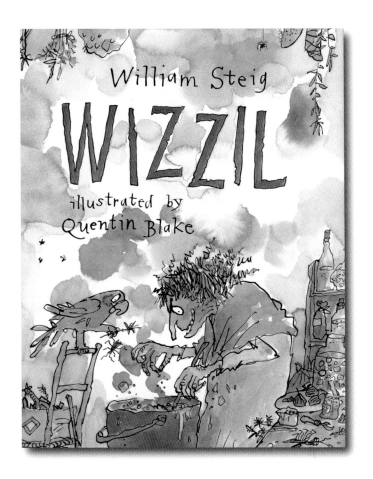

C H A P T E R   1
Wizzil

By William Steig.
Quentin Blake, illustrator.
Farrar, Straus, Giroux, New York: 2000.

Another good read: *Gorky Rises* by William Steig

THE STORY:

Your kids will giggle at the antics of Wizzil, the bored witch looking to make someone else miserable for a change. She chooses the unsuspecting Farmer Frimp as her victim and vows to make him "sizzle." She transforms herself into an unswattable fly, then a mischievous glove for Frimp to wear. The more irritable Wizzil gets, the more things start to fall apart at the house of Farmer Frimp!

You can use this story to illustrate the idea of what happens when things explode — both literally and metaphorically. Your child will actually make water fizz using Alka-Seltzer and water at different temperatures. And your child will certainly be able to identify with anger that seethes so much it makes you want to explode.

You might, for example, ask your child to recall a time that she was that mad. What would she have done if she had Wizzil's powers?

• •

THE SCIENCE:

Pop your top!

In this experiment, as most of us know, when Alka-Seltzer mixes with water, a chemical reaction occurs. The bubbling and fizzing inside the film canister is carbon dioxide gas forming. As the gas builds, the pressure on the lid grows. Eventually, the amount of gas inside the canister becomes larger than the space, and that in turn forces the lid to pop off.

In the second part of the experiment, you will notice that the temperature of the water affects the rate at which the reaction occurs. Colder water slows down the reaction time, while hotter water increases it, so carbon dioxide gas is produced faster, thus causing the lid to "pop off" more quickly.

A look inside those bubbles:

Carbon Dioxide, whose scientific notation is CO_2, comes in many forms. When it is at room temperature in gas form, it's inside the bubbles in your Alka-Seltzer, and it's also what makes your soda or sparkling water fizzy! That's why we call those drinks "carbonated" beverages. Pop Rocks candy also contains little CO_2 bubbles that pop when they mix with the liquids in your mouth. Animals and microorganisms actually produce carbon dioxide when they breathe out. Plants, meanwhile, take in CO_2 during photosynthesis. When you pour water on dry ice, it starts to change — but instead of becoming a liquid, it releases a fog-like gas, which is — you guessed it — CO_2!

THE EXPERIMENT & what you'll need:

- Two Fuji film canisters with interlocking lids (these have the tightest seal)
- Four Alka-Seltzer tablets
- Thermometer
- Stopwatch
- Metric measuring cup (available in drug stores and hospital pharmacies)
- ½ cup cold water with ice cubes
- ½ cup tap water at room temperature
- ½ cup boiling water

1. Introduce the idea. Drop one whole tablet of Alka-Seltzer into a glass of water at room temperature to observe the fizzing tablet making carbon dioxide gas. Describe what you see.

2. Start over, this time ready to experiment. Pour 20mL (milliliters or 4 teaspoons) of tap water into the metric measuring cup.

3. Place the thermometer into the water for one minute and take a temperature reading. Use your stopwatch as your timer.

4. Mark your temperature reading on your data sheet under the Tap water test section. (See p. 28.)

5. Open the top of the film canister and carefully open a package of Alka-Seltzer. Place one whole tablet next to the canister.

6. Pour the 20mL (milliliters or 4 teaspoons) of room-temperature tap water into the canister. Place the lid, canister, and 1 Alka-Seltzer tablet next to each other.

7. Set your stop watch to 00:00.

8. Drop the Alka-Seltzer tablet into the canister, and close it quickly. Start the stopwatch as soon as the top is on the canister.

9. Stop the timer when the lid pops off. This is your reaction time. Note the reaction time on your data sheet.

10. Pour out the contents and rinse and dry the canister.

11. Repeat steps 1-10 using cold water and ice.

12. Repeat steps 1-10 using boiling water

TALKING IT OVER:

Now that your child has noted the various outcomes, you can talk about science and fiction. Here are a few questions you can start with:

What happened when Alka-Seltzer and water are mixed inside a film canister?

What was happening inside the canisters after the lids popped off?

What happened when you increased the temperature of the water? What happened when you decreased it?

Which lid traveled higher in the air? Why?

What could Wizzil have done to Mr. Frimp if she had turned herself into Alka-Seltzer inside a film canister? What would she do to pop more quickly? More slowly?

TAKE IT FURTHER:

- Have your child reduce the size of the Alka-Seltzer tablet by breaking it in half or into quarters to see if that alters the reaction time.
- Observe how the reaction time changes if the Alka-Seltzer tablet is turned into a powder.
- Alka-Seltzer is a great tool for demonstrating other scientific principles as well. Check out the Student Scientific Experiments page at: http://www.alkaseltzer.com/as/experiment/student_experiment.htm.

· ·

WIZZIL DATA SHEET

	Tap water Trial #1	Cold water Trial #2	Cold water Trial #3
Starting temperature of the water			
Time it took for lid to pop off (reaction time)			
How far lid traveled (in feet and inches)			

28

CHAPTER 2
Strega Nona

By Tomie dePaola
Simon and Schuster, New York: 1975.

Another good read: *Spaghetti Eddie* by Ryan Sanangelo

THE STORY:

Your little witch or warlock will yearn to twirl pasta after reading the tale of Strega Nona, which is Italian for "Grandma Witch." The story's beloved Calabrian sorceress provides potions that can cure aches, remove warts and even attract husbands. But the pasta she conjures up in her magical clay cauldron is perhaps her best-kept secret. That is, until her helper Big Anthony is unable to resist the temptation of the pot's magic. One day, when Strega Nona is away, Anthony invites the villagers to come see the enchanted pot and eat the wondrous noodles. But he knows only half of the spell and cannot stop the noodles from taking on a life of their own as they bubble over, out the door, and into the village streets.

Using this story, let your child bring pasta alive using a simple recipe to create a basic chemical reaction similar to the Alka-Selzter procedure in Chapter 1. For fun, he can also come up with a special incantation and demonstrate his "magic" to friends and family members. This activity also provides an opportunity for your child to practice his skills of observation and measurement.

. . . .

THE SCIENCE:

Make your spaghetti "dance"

Vinegar is not just sour wine. Its key ingredient is acetic acid, which reacts when mixed with baking soda (sodium bicarbonate), which is a base. This is called an acid-base reaction. These two household substances combined produce carbon dioxide gas in the form of bubbles. They also produce a solution of sodium acetate, or salt and water. (For more on acid-base reactions, see below.)

In this experiment, the carbon dioxide gas bubbles will stick to the surface of the pasta, and that will cause the pasta to move toward the top of the jar. This occurs because the spaghetti and the gas are both less dense than the water. When the pasta reaches the top of the solution, many of the bubbles pop. As the bubbles disappear, the pasta's density returns to normal and, simply put, the spaghetti will sink because there are no more bubbles to buoy it.

The abcs of acids and bases

Acids and bases are essentially substances at opposite ends of the pH spectrum that cause a reaction when they come in contact with one another. Acids are often sour and will cause a stinging sensation on broken skin. They also cause metal to corrode. As you might imagine, acidic substances include fruit juices, vinegar, wine, carbonated beverages, aspirin solution, and coffee.

Bases, meanwhile, are substances that, if mixed with acids, can neutralize them. Bases often have a soapy feel, slippery to the touch, and a bitter taste, and they are also known as "alkali." Examples of bases include baking soda solution, liquid soaps, bleach, egg whites, crushed egg shells, ammonia, and most stomach remedies like Milk of Magnesia.

In an acid-base reaction, the two types of liquids, when in equal amounts and strengths, can neutralize each other and create water, carbon dioxide, and salt as by-products. This is why, when you have a stomach ache — i.e., too much acidity in your stomach — you might take Milk of Magnesia.

Chemically speaking, acids and bases are so described based on the concentration of hydrogen ions (pH) in the liquid. Acids have a low pH of 6 or less, while bases have a high pH level of 8 or more. Pure and distilled water both have a neutral pH level of 7. The pH level matters because a liquid with a high concentration of hydrogen ions will want to donate — or get rid of — its hydrogen ions, and a base will want to take in those extra hydrogen ions. That is how they neutralize one another and create water in the process.

THE EXPERIMENT & what you'll need:

- Dried pasta noodles or angel hair spaghetti
- Tall glass jar or glass
- Tap water
- ½ cup vinegar
- Baking soda
- Measuring cups and spoons
- Optional: raisins, dried cranberries, pennies

1. Fill a glass jar ⅔ full with water. Leave some open space at the top.

2. Add 1 tablespoon of baking soda to the water. Stir to dissolve the powder.

3. Take four or five pieces of uncooked pasta noodles and break them into ½-inch-long pieces.

4. Put all of the spaghetti into the jar. Observe the jar, and have your child observe what happens to the pasta.

5. Stir the pasta.

6. Measure two tablespoons of vinegar, and add it to the cup. Watch the pasta carefully. If the pasta does not "dance," add ½ tablespoon of vinegar until the pasta starts moving.

TALKING IT OVER:

This experiment is short and sweet, so the best way to help your child understand the science is to slow down, ask questions and get him to observe and reflect every step of the way. Repeating this experiment several times will help your child to observe the reaction more closely. Here are a few good questions:

Before you start: Could Strega Nona really have a magical pasta pot that makes instant, oozing pasta? How would pasta in the magical pot act?

After step 2: What does the water look like when you add the baking soda to it? What does the water look like after the baking soda dissolves?

After step 3, with the broken pasta bits in hand: Can pasta really move or dance without anyone touching it? Give him time to think about the question and come up with a response.

After step 4, as the pasta dances: Describe what is happening to the spaghetti. What is it doing? What else do you see happening in the water? Why do you think this is happening? Why does your spaghetti rise and sink?

TAKE IT FURTHER:

- Your child can also try making other small items "dance." Try it with raisins, pennies or dried cranberries. He can also alter the experiment by placing the pasta pieces in the jar with clear, carbonated beverages like 7-Up, Ginger Ale, Club Soda or Sprite. In this case, the pasta will still "dance" for about five seconds, before the carbonation dissipates.
- To build on the theme of the magic pasta pot, try making a pasta pool! Invite a few friends over and ask each to bring a gallon-size bag of cooked pasta. Have enough pasta on hand to fill a small child's swimming pool. The smallest pools out there usually hold about six gallons. Allow your child and his/her friends to "swim" in pasta to help them understand what happened to the village when Big Anthony could not remember how to break the spell. Make sure to have a hose nearby!

- Another use for the pool of pasta, or any noodles if you have leftovers: Pasta painting! Dip a piece of cooked pasta in tempera paint and use it as a paint brush to create a scene from *Strega Nona*.
- Try the pasta pool on a smaller scale: Make up a small batch of spaghetti and then recreate Big Anthony's pasta disaster, using little people in Lego houses or shoebox structures, for example.

• •

SCIENTIST'S NOTEBOOK FOR *STREGA NONA*

Use this page to paint with pasta, or recreate a scene from Strega Nona. *You can also record your notes from the experiment or draw pictures of the dancing spaghetti, coins, raisins, etc.*

NOTES:

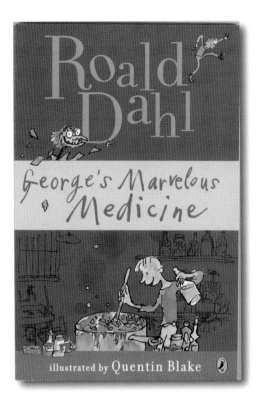

CHAPTER 3
George's Marvelous Medicine

By Roald Dahl.
Quentin Blake, illustrator.
Penguin Putnam, New York: 1981.

Other good reads: *Good Magic, Spells, Potions and More from History, Literature & Make-Believe* by Carole Marsh; and *Mrs. Piggle-Wiggle's Magic* by Betty Macdonald (for younger readers)

THE STORY:

Eight-year-old George Kranky lives with a bully: His grandma. One day, when he is left alone with her, he decides to concoct a cure for her meanness. Instead of giving her the usual spoonful of medicine, George pours bucketfuls of toxic household products into a bubbling cauldron — from leg hair remover to purple horse pills, anti-freeze, paraffin, and brown shoe polish. Sure enough, Grandma swallows George's nasty brew and proceeds to breathe clouds of smoke, bulge up, turn green and purple, then sprout up like a beanstalk.

When George's farmer father sees what has happened, he wants George to recreate his potion so he can grow giant livestock and make money. But George did not write down his recipe, and after four attempts cannot create a monster chicken. (Still, the fourth potion does manage to make Grandma disappear.)

Let your child try to recreate George's marvelous medicine — under your supervision and far from the lips of Grandma or any unsuspecting sibling! Using purple cabbage and water (rather than truly toxic chemicals), she can make a wonderful purple potion that will change colors as it is mixed with common household liquids. But she should remember to write down the recipes if she wants to duplicate the experiment later on! As off-putting as we might consider the idea of poisoning granny, your child may love imagining a potion that can make a bully smoke and sputter and balloon up, then wither away.

● ●

THE SCIENCE:

Boiling up a witchy brew, then changing the color!

In this experiment, you will start by creating a purple cabbage juice solution. The skin of cabbage contains a pigment molecule called anthocyanin, which is also found in plants such as roses and cornflowers as well as fruits like plums, grapes, and red apples. In fact, anthocyanin gives these plant parts their deep red coloring. Purple cabbage has a particularly high concentration of anthocyanin, which is a natural substance that is used to determine the pH level of liquids. Basically, purple cabbage juice can be used to tell if a liquid or solution is an acid, neutral, or base.

Purple cabbage juice is an indicator solution. The color of the cabbage juice solution changes in response to changes in its hydrogen ion concentration. Foods like lemon juice, lime juice, and vinegar are acids. When acids mix with the indicator, the cabbage juice turns from purple to pink in color.

Other substances like baking soda, liquid soap, and ammonia are bases. These liquids also cause a color change in the indicator. Purple cabbage juice is changed to bluish-green color when mixed with a base. If a liquid is a neutral, like distilled water, there will be no alteration to the purple cabbage juice's color.

THE EXPERIMENT & what you'll need:

- One gallon distilled water
- One head of purple cabbage
- Blender
- Strainer
- 7 small disposable cups
- ½ cup lemon juice
- ½ cup vinegar
- ½ cup ammonia
- ½ cup baking soda solution (water and baking soda)
- ½ cup lime juice
- ½ cup salt water
- Measuring cups
- One bowl or large container
- Marking pen
- ½ cup liquid soap solution: mix 1 cup water to 15 ml or 1 Tbsp of dishwashing liquid

A note about the ingredients:

Do the experiment immediately after you've poured the liquids into the little cups. Exposure to impurities in the air will cause changes to the indicator (the purple cabbage juice) and make it less effective at determining pH levels. If you have to wait 1 to 8 hours before completing the experiment, keep the indicator in a sealed container.

SAFETY ALERT

Explain to your child that she is about to use household liquids in the kitchen to create a color-changing potion like George did in the story. *Note: It is unsafe to taste any "medicine" he or she creates in this experiment!*

1.   Pull the leaves off the head of cabbage. Break the leaves into small pieces and put them in the blender.

2.   Fill the blender halfway with about 3 to 4 cups of warm distilled water.

3.   Blend the water and cabbage on high for 2 minutes. What does the solution look like?

    Hint: it should be dark purple with small pieces of leaves floating around.

4.   Strain the liquid from the mixture, using a strainer and capturing the purple juice in a bowl or another container. Throw out the remaining cabbage pulp and set the juice aside.

5   Using a marker, label the seven cups as follows: cabbage juice, lemon juice, vinegar, ammonia, baking soda solution, soap solution, and lime juice.

6. Now, write the name of each liquid on your data sheet. This is where you will keep track of your recipe and its results, unlike George did.

7. Pour ¼ cup of cabbage juice into each of the labeled cups.

8. Have your child jot down the color of the cabbage juice.

9. Using a clean measuring cup, add ¼ cup of lemon juice to the proper cup. What happens to the cabbage juice when you mix in the lemon juice?

(**Hint:** it should turn pink!) Write it down on your data sheet. Think about it: Why did the cabbage juice change color when you added lemon juice?

10. Repeat steps above for the six remaining cups using the appropriate liquid. Remember to observe and write down the color changes you see.

CONNECTING SCIENCE WITH FICTION:

Here are a few questions to bring it back to the book:

Did George really make medicine?

Did George's grandma change colors after she took the magic medicine? Can you name a few?

Is it possible to make a liquid change colors? What are a few ways to do this?

Hint: Remember how colors changed in the Oobleck experiment? What did George do to change the color of his potion?

Have your child create a diagram of all four of George's recipes. After writing down the ingredients, note what each recipe does to its recipient's shape and size. This will reinforce the notion that slight changes in a recipe can cause very different results. Note the importance of following a recipe as closely as possible.

TAKE IT FURTHER:

- Allow your child time to find other liquids in the kitchen to test and record their findings. You can turn ½ cup of any powder (sugar, salt, cream of tartar, cornstarch) into a solution by mixing it with ½ cup of distilled water.

 Hint: You will need to lighten dark liquids like coffee and sodas by adding distilled water before testing. This will not affect their pH levels.

- If you get hooked on testing liquids in purple cabbage juice, you can mix ¼ cup of a known acid with ¼ cup of a known base. Then add the solution to ½ cup of purple cabbage juice solution. The base and acid will have neutralized, and the cabbage juice will remain purple.

- Try making indicators from other things. What other vegetables will give you a good strong color? How about beets or the leaves of marigolds or hydrangea? Do they react with acids and alkalis in the same way?

- Introduce your young chemist to the pH scale. Go to a pool supply or pet store and purchase pH strips. Your child can find out the exact strength of her acids and bases using the strips.

- Have your child check her data from this experiment by going to The pH Factor at the Miami Museum of Science's website: http://www.miamisci.org/ph/index.html. This site allows your child to play chemist in the virtual lab as they learn about acids and bases.

GEORGE'S MARVELOUS MEDICINE DATA SHEET

Liquid Number	Test Liquids	Color change of purple cabbage indicator	Is this liquid an acid, base or neutral?
1. Lemon juice			
2. Vinegar			
3. Ammonia			
4. Baking soda solution			
5. Lime juice			
6. Liquid dishwashing soap			
7. Salt water			

43

 Hint: use the information in "The Science" section, p. 38, to help you determine whether the liquid is an acid base or neutral.

NOTES:

44

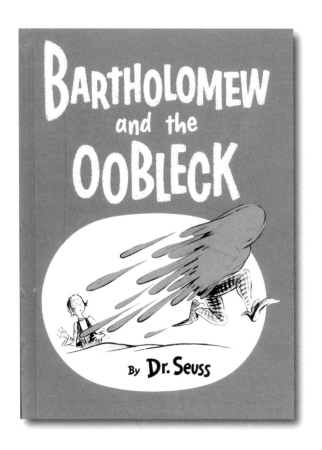

C H A P T E R 4

Bartholomew and the Oobleck

By Dr. Seuss.
Random House, New York: 1949.

Other good reads: *A Weird Case of Super-Goo* by Kenneth Oppel; *Gobs of Goo* by Vicki Cobb.

THE STORY:

In this delightful book by Dr. Seuss, the King of Didd awakes one morning growling at the sky, whose sun, rain, fog and snow are far too predictable for his taste. He orders his trusted page boy, Bartholomew, to summon the royal magicians, certain that they can create something entirely new and exciting. The royal magicians set out to create a green gel-like substance they call Oobleck. But the king soon learns to be careful what he wishes for. As greenish "clouds" blanket the kingdom and bury the magicians' cave with the goo, the king is the only person who can undo the spell, but he must figure out what the magic words are.

Your child will relish the role of royal magician, recreating red, blue, green and yellow versions of the globules that rain down upon the Kingdom of Didd. And while the king's magicians fed a fire with ingredients such as wet mouse hair, yellow twigs, a sour lizard skin and a stocking full of dust, your magician will use household glue and food coloring, and won't go near any flames!

THE SCIENCE:

Concocting colorful, sticky & gooey stuff!

What the magicians of Didd were creating, and what your child will create, is a soft-matter substance known as a polymer. Polymers are often thought of as plastics, but in fact many polymers are naturally occurring, such as rubber, the proteins that make up human hair and nails, and cellulose, which makes up wood and plant leaves and stems.

By creating multiple polymers based upon one recipe, which is also sometimes called GLUEp, your child will learn how slight differences in the amount of one ingredient can change their physical properties.

The polymer that your child will create is a synthetic polymer. The glue base she will use contains hundreds of polymers floating freely in the liquid. When mixed with the sodium borate solution made from 20 Mule Team Borax (which is a binding agent), the polymer molecules will lock together and become semi-solid. The amount of water added to the mixture will affect how tightly the chains of polymers can link together. The more water added to the recipe, the more the polymer can "stretch," the less it can bounce and the more poorly it retains its shape.

What is a Polymer?

A **polymer** is essentially a large molecule, often containing many thousands of small molecules joined together chemically to form one giant **macromolecule**. Its name comes from the Greek words meaning "many parts." As discussed, some polymers are naturally occurring (as in cellulose and the proteins that form bird feathers and human hair), but many — such as Oobleck and slime — are synthetic.

The synthetic polymer you are most familiar with is plastic. Glue is another polymer, as are styrofoam and nylon. People can mix together a variety of chemicals to tie together these free-floating, long chains of molecules through a process called "cross-linking." Cross–linking helps to tie all the polymer molecules together thus creating one giant molecule that is strong, somewhat flexible, and not easily broken. You can sometimes spot a polymer by its name: If it ends in —"on", like nylon or rayon, it can be a polymer. Or if it begins with "poly", like polyester or polystyrene, it is one.

In the four experiments that follow, the first (Red Oobleck) as the control does not list water as an ingredient. This allows your young scientist to observe how the addition of water changes the outcome.

THE EXPERIMENT & what you'll need:

- White glue (Elmer's Glue works best)
- Food coloring – yellow, red, blue and green
- Spoons
- 4 mixing bowls
- Metric medicine measuring cup, measuring spoons
- 2 cups 20 Mule Team Borax laundry powder
- Tap water

Red Oobleck

- 15 mL (milliliters or 1 Tbsp) glue
- 2 drops red food coloring
- 10 mL (2 tsp) sodium borate solution

Green Oobleck

- 15 mL (1 Tbsp) glue
- 2 drops green food coloring
- 5 mL (1 tsp) water
- 10 mL sodium borate solution

Yellow Oobleck

- 15 mL (1 Tbsp) glue
- 2 drops yellow food coloring
- 15 mL (1 Tbsp) water
- 10 mL (2 tsp) sodium borate solution

Blue Oobleck

- 15 mL (1 Tbsp) glue
- 2 drops blue food coloring
- 30 mL (2 Tbsp) water
- 10 mL (2 tsp) sodium borate solution

1. **Make the sodium borate solution the day before doing the experiments. Follow these easy steps with or without your child's help:**

   • Mix two cups of 20 Mule Team Borax with two liters (two quarts) of hot water in a bottle or pitcher.
   • Shake the solution well.
   • You will notice chunks of Borax resting in the bottle. This is normal, since the water cannot hold any additional Borax.
   • Allow the solution to set overnight.
   • Shake well before using.

2. Choose which Oobleck to make first, but make the blue Oobleck last as it is the most runny and least "malleable."

3. Measure 15mL or 1 Tbsp of glue and pour it into a cup or mixing bowl.

4. Add two drops of food coloring to the glue and stir it until it is completely blended.

5. Measure water (if applicable) in a clean measuring cup, then pour it into the glue/food coloring mixture and stir until well-blended.

6. Measure the sodium borate solution and slowly pour it into the mixture as your child stirs for about one minute.

7. Lift the spoon slowly out of the mixing cup or bowl to observe the Oobleck.

8. Pull the Oobleck off the spoon and remove any leftovers from the cup.

9. Knead the Oobleck in your hands for another minute or more.

10. Place the Oobleck in an airtight bag to preserve it, and see how the different colors react when tested.

11. Repeat steps #1-10 with the different-colored Oobleck recipes.

TALKING IT OVER:

As your child manipulates the different Ooblecks, she will notice their different physical properties. Ask her to record how each version of Oobleck acts on her data sheet. Later, you can analyze the information and compare results.

What does this polymer look like?

See if you can stretch it with both hands.

Can you roll this polymer into a ball?

If so, watch it closely and observe

　1. Will it retain its shape when placed on a table?

Or

　2. Will it flatten after two minutes?

Once it's rolled up in a ball, can you roll it across the floor?

Now you can experiment and see how many times you can make it bounce. Try throwing it down harder. What happens?

GET CREATIVE:

After you're done experimenting with the different forms and colors of oobleck, have your child retell the story of *Bartholomew and the Oobleck*, replacing Dr. Seuss's oobleck with the polymers he or she has created.

Have her draw pictures of the Kingdom of Didd if red, blue or yellow oobleck had fallen from the sky. She can even create details within her drawing that represent the "behavior" of each polymer, for example, bouncing red oobleck or slimy blue oobleck oozing through the town.

TAKE IT FURTHER:

- Let your child play chemist. She can develop her own Oobleck recipe by changing one ingredient. Scientists in a lab would change only one ingredient at a time, so that's what your child should do. Once she has made a new Oobleck, have her test it and add her data to the chart for analysis.
- For more fun with polymers, check out "Paul Lemur's Tree House" at http://pslc.ws/macrog/paul/, which is full of interactive games, videos, an online coloring book and self-quizzes.
- Copy the following sheet and use it for each version of Oobleck. You may use check marks or color in the boxes. Then compare data sheets.

• •

BARTHOLOMEW AND THE OOBLECK DATA SHEET

Test performed on _____ Oobleck	Yes	Somewhat (does it, but not well)	No	Comments
1. Roll Oobleck into a ball. Does it keep its shape?				
2. Pat Oobleck between your hands and try to form a thin film. Does it stay thin?				
3. Drop a ball of Oobleck on a table. Does it bounce?				
4. Use a penny to make imprints in the Oobleck. Does the imprint of the penny stay on the Oobleck?				
5. Roll the Oobleck into a worm shape and slowly pull it apart while holding both ends. Does it tear easily?				
6. Reform the worm shape, and pull it apart quickly. Does it tear easily?				
7. Using a washable marker, write your name on a plastic bag. Shape the Oobleck into a small pancake, place it over the design, and remove it carefully. Does your name appear on the Oobleck?				
8. Reform the pancake, place it on a piece of newspaper and remove it carefully. Does the newsprint appear on the Oobleck?				

52

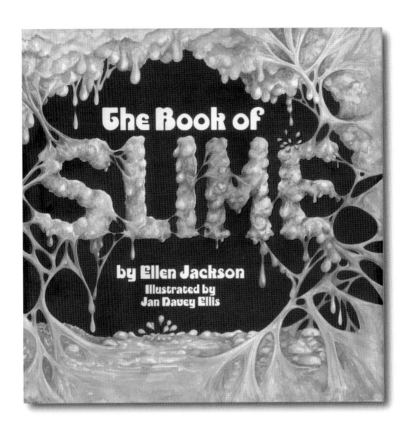

CHAPTER 5
The Book of Slime

By Ellen Jackson.
Jan Davey Ellis, illustrator.
Millbrook Press, Brookfield, CN: 1997.

Other good reads: *The Slime Wars* by Debbie Dandy,
It's True! We Came from Slime by Ken McNamara

THE STORY:

Whether your child loves playing with slimy stuff or squeals with disgust at its mere mention, she will learn everything she needs to know about slime in this primer. Believe it or not, nature uses slippery, gooey, goopy substances like raw egg whites and snail ooze to help plants, animals, and people. Uncover the fun and fictional side of slime through stories, edible recipes (slime pie!); and jokes (Q: Who won the slimy monster beauty contest? A: No one).

· ·

THE SCIENCE:

Create something slimy!

In this experiment, you and your child will make a cornstarch polymer with a slimy texture. The 18th century scientist and mathematician Sir Isaac Newton discovered that most liquids flow quickly when heated, and they will thicken and resist movement when cooled. Not so with the slimy polymer you will make, which is classified as a "non-Newtonian fluid."

Non-Newtonian fluids can look and feel like both liquids and solids, but their flow — or viscosity — only changes when you change the type of pressure you apply to its surface. For example, the water molecules and the cornstarch contained in your slime will become snarled when you press on it directly and swiftly. This will cause it to resist flowing and behave more like a solid. However, when you lighten your touch, move on an angle, or move slowly, the molecules in the polymer will behave more like liquid; thus, flowing and wavering like a liquid.

To understand what we mean by polymer, please read "What is a Polymer?" p. 47.

54

What's lurking in your refrigerator?

Explore the kitchen with your child after reading *The Book of Slime*. Look closely at cooked spaghetti, the uncooked whites of eggs, warm butter, jello, puddings, and gravies and sauces. (But not so much that she gets grossed out by dinner!) Prepare half-cups of these foods and guide her through this exercise with gentle questions:

What words can you use to describe this food?

Is it a liquid or a solid?

How does it feel and move? How does it "behave"?

Is it slime? Or just slimy?

Now you are ready to create an edible slime that will allow both of you to explore the properties of liquids and solids found in a non-Newtonian fluid.

Once your child's concoction is ready, have her describe the texture and taste of this edible polymer. Be prepared for squeals of delight or groans of horror as this dry feeling, semi-liquid lands in her hands.

THE EXPERIMENT & what you'll need:

- 6 Tbsps cornstarch
- 3 Tbsps tap water
- Mixing bowl
- Food coloring (green works well!)
- Measuring spoons
- A few drops of liquid flavoring (any flavor you like)
- One large spoon
- 2 small cups

55

1. Pour four tablespoons of cornstarch into a mixing bowl.

2. Stir two drops of food coloring into the cornstarch.

3. Stir in one teaspoon of liquid flavoring. The cornstarch will encapsulate the flavoring and coloring as you mix it into the powder.

4. Slowly stir two tablespoons of tap water into the cornstarch mixture.

5. The mixture will begin to look and flow like a liquid and then "act" like a solid when you touch it with a spoon or your finger — which brings us back to its place as a "non-Newtonian" fluid (see "The Science" section above). If it does not form a smooth, non-lumpy surface, add one tablespoon of water until you attain the right consistency. There should be no lumps and no cornstarch powder remaining.

6. If it becomes too watery or does not look like a solid, add a pinch of cornstarch and stir. (Note: This polymer usually requires a 2:1 ratio of cornstarch to water.)

7. Once properly mixed, quickly and firmly touch the surface of the mixture with your finger or the bottom of the spoon. It should feel hard, like a solid. Your finger will not go through the surface of the polymer.

8. Now gently tap the surface of the mixture, which is now a "cornstarch polymer." Waves and ripples should form. If you slowly slide your finger downward, you should observe slight ripples.

9. Pour the slimy cornstarch polymer back and forth between the two small cups. You may be surprised that it pours like liquid water but flows more slowly.

10. Over the kitchen sink or outside, pour this cornstarch polymer into your child's hands. As the polymer flows through her fingers, allow her to taste the polymer.

Important: Put any remaining cornstarch polymer into a resealable bag or container for disposal. Do NOT put it down a sink or storm drain. IT WILL CLOG YOUR PIPES!

TAKE IT FURTHER

- Other non-Newtonian fluids can be found in your kitchen and ready for your child to explore. Give your child ½ cup of ketchup or honey to "play" with. Honey and ketchup contain natural polymers and are non-Newtonian fluids. Have your child compare how their slime, ketchup, and honey move and behave. Chart their discovery on a dry erase board or construction paper.
- Click on You Tube (www.youtube.com) for films demonstrating the properties of non-Newtonian fluids. You should preview films prior to watching with your child, since some will be inappropriate for children.

57

THE BOOK OF SLIME SCIENTIST'S DATA SHEET

Use this page to take notes on your slime making, or draw slimy pictures!

PART II

Fun with Food Science

NOTES:

60

C H A P T E R   6
The Butter Battle Book

By Dr. Seuss,
Random House, New York: 1984.

Other good reads: *Let's Make Butter*
by Eleanor Christian and Lyzz Roth-Singer

THE STORY:

Your child may not recognize the Cold-War references in this book about the Yooks and their sworn enemies, the Zooks, but you surely will. Separated by a wall, the two sides battle over whether to butter bread upside down or "butter side up." As the conflict escalates, so do the weapons, and a simple slingshot soon gives way to the Eight-Nozzled, Elephant-Toted Boom-Blitz. The end of this arms race produces a nerve-wracking standstill, as both sides have managed to produce the deadliest weapon of all, the Bitsy Big-Boy Boomeroo. Rather than resolve the conflict, Dr. Seuss leaves us to ponder what will occur to these two civilizations if they use their highly destructive weapons against each other.

After reading such a tale, there's not much to do except learn how to turn cream into butter. But don't stop there! Make small changes to the basic butter recipe to see if temperature and time changes affect how this gel colloid forms. Then have a taste test: Which butter is best, and which side of the bread tastes better?

THE SCIENCE:

Shake cream into butter!

All cream has proteins and fat globules in it. When you and your child shake the cream, the fat globules stick together and form butter. The remaining liquid part, called buttermilk, has the proteins and can also be consumed.

In the second butter recipe, the cream that you leave out of the refrigerator for 12 hours will have a different texture and taste from the cold cream butter. The fat globules in the warm cream will form crystals. These crystals will burst the membranes that will form around each fat globule as you shake the jar. As these membranes burst during shaking, the warm cream butter will form a smoother and larger solid of butter. Letting the cream sit at room temperature allows lactic acid, a good bacteria, to grow. Lactic acid not only gives the warm cream butter a richer and stronger taste, it helps prevent the growth of bacteria that could be harmful to humans.

THE EXPERIMENT & what you'll need:

- 2 pints heavy cream
- 2 small plastic containers with airtight lids or 2 baby food jars
- Stopwatch or kitchen timer
- 1 clean marble
- Salt
- Several slices of bread or crackers
- Butter knife

A Note on Timing:

You will probably want to have both butters on hand for taste tests, so try to have both butters ready at the same time. Since Butter recipe #2 needs to sit out for 12 hours, you might consider setting out the cream the night before, on weekends, or at breakfast for an evening experiment.

In Butter recipe #1, shaking the cream might get a little boring after 20 minutes. Try singing your way through it. To the tune of "Row, Row, Row Your Boat," sing: "Shake, Shake, Shake your cream/Turn it into butter. Shake it fast, and shake it slow to make the lumps of butter." Or perhaps: "100 globules of Cream in the Jar, 100 Globules of Cream. Shake it well to help make it jell, 99 globules of cream in the Jar." Make up words to all your favorite songs. And then think about how nice it is that we can hop in the car to buy butter at the store!

Butter recipe #1

1. Measure one pint of cold heavy cream and pour it into the jar or plastic container. The jar should have a tight-fitting lid.

2. Add one clean marble to the jar, then close it.

3. Shake the jar for 20 minutes or until lumps of fat and protein form. You and your child can take turns.

4. Once the butter has formed (you will notice large lumps), pour off the excess liquid remaining in the jar. This is buttermilk.

5. Mix a pinch of salt into the butter lumps.

6. Spread the butter on bread or crackers with a butter knife and enjoy!

7. Refrigerate the remaining butter for a comparison test later.

Butter recipe #2

1. Measure one pint of heavy cream and let it sit out, at room temperature, for about 12 hours.

2. Once it has sat, pour it into a glass jar or plastic container. This time, no marble is needed because you won't need as much friction to make the globules join together. Put the lid on the jar, and do not worry if the cream has a slightly sour smell.

3. Shake the jar once and stop. Observe what is happening to the warm cream inside the jar.

4. Continue to give the jar a good hard shake about once every second.

5. Observe the cream carefully. For the first few minutes, you will not notice much happening. Then suddenly you'll feel a solid hitting the jar when you shake it. Look inside and you should see a large lump of butter. Give it a few more hard jolts and the butter will be ready.

6. Open the jar and observe. Once again, liquid buttermilk will be in the jar with the solid butter.

7. Pour off the buttermilk and add one tablespoon of very cold water to the jar. Swirl it around a bit, and then pour it off.

8. Repeat this rinsing of the butter, until the water remains clear.

9. Drain all the water and put the lump of butter into a small bowl. Again, add a pinch of salt, or the same amount you added to the cold cream butter.

10. Take the cold cream butter out of the refrigerator for the taste tests.

TALKING IT OVER:

Dr. Seuss' surreal tale will give you an opening to discuss silly conflicts and how they can escalate. The butter recipe will inject some fun and food into the more serious topic of how sometimes fights can get out of hand over an inconsequential detail.

After reading the book, ask your child why the Zooks and the Yooks are fighting in *The Butter Battle Book*. Reinforce the idea that the two sides couldn't agree on how to eat buttered bread.

Ask your child if he knows how butter is made. Talk about foods that change from liquids to solids when heated, frozen, shaken, or beaten such as egg whites when whipped to form peaks or cream when whipped to form whipped cream.

Before making the second butter recipe, have your child talk about what might be different if you make it with cream that is not cold. How might its taste, texture, and appearance differ?

Once the two butters are made, hold a taste test to determine which butter — and buttering method, of course — is the tastiest.

Your child should describe the differences in appearance, taste, and texture between the two types of butter and note them in his scientist's notebook.

Finally, ask your child what he thinks will happen to the Yooks and the Zooks. Have him re-write or re-tell the story and

65

develop an ending from the perspective of both the Yooks and the Zooks. What if both sides were to conclude that it didn't matter how you buttered your bread? Your child can also role-play his story for you if he does not want to complete the writing task.

TAKE IT FURTHER:

- If your child gets hooked on butter-making, have him explore the concept of milk fat in butter by trying to create butter with Half & Half, powdered milk, or whole milk. If the milk has been homogenized, it will not form cream.
- Your child will notice that "homemade" butter is paler than store-bought butter. Coloring has been added to commercial butter. Your little chef can also experiment with the color of butter by adding drops of food coloring to the cream before shaking it. He can make multiple colors of butter, then keep a chart of which family members and friends prefer which color. Which color would the Zooks prefer, and which would the Yooks eat?
- Take your child to a local dairy farm so he can observe where milk and cream come from. Or check out "The Story of Milk" at www.moomilk.com for a virtual tour from the cow's udders to the refrigerator.

THE BUTTER BATTLE BOOK SCIENTIST'S NOTEBOOK

Use this page to record your tasting notes and determine which butter is the tastiest. Record appearance (color) as well as texture of each one.

NOTES:

CHAPTER 7
Chocolate Fever

By Robert Kimmel Smith.
Gioia Fiammenghi, illustrator.
Penguin Putnum Group. New York: 1998.

Other good reads: *Chocolatina* by Erik Kraft; *Smart About
Chocolate: A Sweet History* by Charise Mericle Harper

THE STORY:

Your kids will lick their lips as they read about Henry Green, a boy whose parents let him eat chocolate every day at every meal and every snack. That is... until one day at school when a mysterious rash quickly forms all over his body. The little brown spots make a "pop" as they appear, and Henry starts to smell like — you guessed it — chocolate. When the school nurse rushes Henry to the hospital, Dr. Fargo diagnoses Henry with the only known case of "chocolate fever." Is there a cure, or is Henry doomed to spend his life being made of his favorite food? This is how Henry's quest for a cure begins.

Using Henry's favorite food as an inspiration, your child can explore the melting point of chocolate and create a yummy chocolate drink. The idea is to learn how chocolate melts to understand why hot chocolate sometimes has lumps. Henry would be very pleased to participate in this experiment; at least, he might have been before catching the fever!

THE SCIENCE:

Three ways to let it melt in your mouth!

This experiment is more than just an excuse for your child to chomp on some chocolate. Three techniques for melting the chocolate — on the tongue, moving the tongue, and chewing with teeth — will focus your child's attention on the rate at which chocolate dissolves in saliva. Saliva, of course, is a solvent that contains enzymes that help break down complex carbohydrates like sugar as the food moves around in the mouth. The "solute" (anything that is dissolved) in this experiment is the chocolate. Note that in hot chocolate, the hot milk is the solvent that dissolves the cocoa powder, the solute.

SOLVENTS AND SOLUTES

Why do the pieces of chocolate take a different amount of time to dissolve in her mouth? To answer this, we must first understand how solvents and solutes work. For a solvent to break down a solute, it must be in contact with the surface area of the solute. The more area of the chocolate is exposed to the solvent, the quicker it can break down the chocolate. In the experiment, the only variable was the amount of movement each piece of chocolate experienced while in the mouth.

THE EXPERIMENT, piece by delectable piece.

In **part one**, the piece of chocolate will sit in her mouth and slowly dissolve away. This is just like emptying a packet of cocoa powder into a cup of hot water or milk. Without any movement to expose more surface areas of the solute, it takes a while for the solvent (milk or water) to dissolve the cocoa powder.

In **part two**, she will swish the chocolate around with his tongue. This action mimics the stirring of cocoa powder in the solvent (hot water or milk). It takes less time than just letting it sit there, but it still takes time to expose all the surfaces of the cocoa to the water. This is one reason why your get lumps of cocoa powder in your hot chocolate if you do not stir enough.

Finally, in **part three**, the chocolate will dissolve very quickly because your child will use his teeth to chew up the piece of chocolate. Chewing the chocolate allows the saliva to come in contact with a larger surface area more quickly. This is similar to putting hot water or milk in a blender with cocoa powder. The blades of the blender act like teeth and can quickly break up dry clumps of cocoa powder. This makes hot chocolate much quicker and smooth in texture.

Hint: On the average, chocolate will begin to melt at a temperature of 78 degrees Fahrenheit. That means that the hotter your solvent and the faster you move the cocoa powder, the better your hot chocolate will be.

The Legend of Xocolatl

Chocolate is a beloved ingredient around the world. We eat it in candy bars, milk, cereal, coffee, medicines, and even spicy Mexican sauces! But have you really ever thought about where it came from?

Chocolate originated more than 2,000 years ago in the jungles of Central and South America. The ancient Aztecs and Mayans (and also probably their predecessors) made chocolate from the beans of the prized cacao tree. Legend had it that the Aztec god Quetzalcoatl brought the cacao tree from Paradise to earth, traveling on a beam of the Morning Star. He gave the tree as an offering to the people, and they learned how to roast and grind its beans into a paste. They added spices and mixed it with water, calling it "xocolatl" or "bitterwater." They believed that it brought wisdom and knowledge to those who drank it.

Today cacao is an important agricultural product in the tropics all around the world. Growers from West Africa, South America, East Asia, the Caribbean and some of the Pacific islands produced more than 3 million tons in 1999-2000, and global demand continues to rise. In fact, there is some concern about a shortage of cacao plants because of the destruction of their natural habitat — the rain forest.

CONNECTING SCIENCE WITH FICTION

What would life be like if you broke out in a rash of your favorite food? Would you become Milkshake Mary, Pizza Pam, or Grill Cheesy Stevie? Invent a character and make up a name for the disease. What would the cure be?

THE EXPERIMENT & what you'll need:

- 1 milk chocolate bar broken into three equal pieces
- Stopwatch or watch with a second hand
- Hot water or milk

- Cocoa powder or hot chocolate mix
- Hershey's chocolate kisses, frozen (optional)
- Hungry child

1. She places the first piece of chocolate in her mouth with no chewing or sucking. Once it has dissolved, she opens her mouth and signals the person with the timer to stop the watch.

2. As soon as she places the chocolate in her mouth, start the stopwatch. Do not stop the timer until your child gives you the signal.

3. Record on your data sheet how long it took for that piece of chocolate to dissolve.

4. She places the second piece of chocolate on her tongue. This time, she may move the chocolate around in the mouth using her tongue, but does not chew it.

5. Again, keep time with the stopwatch, announcing the seconds as they go.

6. Again, she opens her mouth once the chocolate has completely melted, says "stop the watch!." Record how long it took to melt.

7. She places the third piece of chocolate on her tongue. This time, chewing it! She opens her mouth once the chocolate has completely melted and records how long it took for the chocolate to dissolve.

8. Compare the times between the three trials. Why do you think the second piece dissolved more quickly than the first? Why did the third dissolve quickest?

9. Explain to your child how solvents and solutes work.

If your child is **hungry for more chocolate**, create hot chocolate following the procedure to dissolve it with parent heating and pouring the milk:

1. Cup #1 – just pour the cocoa powder into hot milk or water.

2. Cup #2 – pour and stir cocoa powder into hot milk or water.

3. Cup #3 – pour cocoa powder into hot milk or water and mix in a blender on high speed for one minute.

4. Keep track of the three cups. How long does it take for the cocoa to dissolve in each of the cups? Record your observations on the data sheet.

5. The best part: Taste the different cups of hot chocolate. Describe the texture of each one. Which one do you prefer? Why?

TAKE IT FURTHER:

- Repeat the candy bar experiment using frozen pieces of chocolate. The challenge: How long will a frozen kiss take to melt in your mouth? Take a guess and write it down on the data sheet. Then take the frozen kisses and repeat steps 1–8. Create a bar or picture graph that illustrates the difference in melting times for a frozen chocolate compared to a non-frozen chocolate.
- The Sweet Science of Chocolate is the Exploratorium's website devoted to all things chocolate. Learn about chocolate's origins in the Amazon rain forest, visit a chocolate factory, and see the amazing things chefs can do with this treat. Go to http://www.exploratorium.edu/chocolate/live.html to get your chocolate fix.
- Check out "Manufacturing Chocolate from Seed to Sweet," an interactive game for children created by the Field Museum in Chicago. Kids learn how chocolate is grown, harvested, processed, and manufactured. See: http://www.fieldmuseum.org/Chocolate/kids_seedtosweet.html.

CHOCOLATE FEVER DATA SHEET

Test #1 – Room temperature chocolate

Temperature of the chocolate bar: _____

	Chocolate sitting on your tongue	Chocolate around by your tongue	Chocolate chewed by your teeth
Time to dissolve			

Test #2 – Hot chocolate and how it dissolves

Temperature of the hot milk: _____

	Cocoa powder: dumped on the hot milk	Cocoa powder: stirred into hot milk	Cocoa powder: put through a blender
Time to dissolve			
How does the cocoa powder appear?			
Describe the texture and taste of the hot chocolate.			

Test #3 – Frozen chocolate

Temperature of the chocolate kiss: _____

	Chocolate sitting on your tongue	Chocolate moved around by your tongue	Chocolate chewed by your teeth
Time to dissolve			

NOTES:

CHAPTER 8
Ice Cream Larry

By Daniel Pinkwater.
Jill Pinkwater, illustrator.
Marshall Cavendish, New York: 1999.

Other good reads: *Ice Cream: The Full Scoop*
by Gail Gibbons; *Ice Cream* by Jules Older;
From Cow to Ice Cream by Bertram T. Knight.

THE STORY:

Your kids will devour the quirky tale of Larry, a Moby Dick-reading polar bear, who lives at the Hotel Larry, where he works, oddly enough, as a lifeguard. One day, Larry, overheated and bored, talks his way into spending the afternoon in the walk-in freezer at Cohen's Cones, the local ice cream shop. Mrs. Cohen is furious to find out he has eaten 250 pounds of ice cream and banishes him. But Larry becomes a worldwide sensation once the media gets hold of the story. Soon, he meets Mr. I. Berg, the owner of the Iceberg Ice Cream company, which made the tubs that Larry consumed inside the freezer. Larry becomes the company spokesman, which of course comes with some ice-cold perks.

While learning about freezing points, you child can play the role of Larry — or Mr. Berg — and make different flavors of ice cream without using an ice cream maker.

. . . .

THE SCIENCE:

Freeze your own ice cream in a can!

It's true: We all scream for ice cream! Americans are the world's most avid consumers of the stuff, slurping down more than 21 quarts annually per capita, according to a 2004 U.S. Department of Agriculture report.

But how much do you know about how ice cream is frozen? In this experiment, your child will take a liquid and freeze it, thereby changing its state to a solid. The secret ingredient is the rock salt added to the crushed ice. Just as salt helps icy roads to thaw in winter, salt mixed with ice in a canister causes its freezing point to decrease and the ice to melt, which eventually results in a soft frozen treat.

How temperature affects ice cream's softness

Normally, water will freeze at 32 degrees Fahrenheit. But when salt is added, the freezing point decreases to around 15 degrees Fahrenheit. The water, which is now salt water, won't freeze until its temperature dips below that. At a lowered temperature, the mixture begins to freeze into crystals, which are quite small and more evenly distributed than regular ice crystals. As long as more ice and salt are added to the larger can, the mixture will continue to freeze. The mixture will not become solid, like an ice cube, because the constant movement of the ice crystals causes them to be evenly distributed. That movement allows air bubbles and even smaller crystals to form, and those crystals are not as rocky and hard as regular ice. This is how ice cream stays soft!

Rock salt is not the only ingredient that lowers the freezing point. Besides making ice cream sweet, sugar also serves another important purpose. In the freezer, plain cream turns into a solid that's as hard as a rock. Sugar lowers the mixture's freezing temperature, making it a much softer product.

THE EXPERIMENT & what you'll need:

- ½ cup of whole milk
- ½ cup of heavy cream
- ½ teaspoon vanilla or other flavoring extract
- ¼ cup of granulated sugar
- 4 cups crushed ice, either store-bought or smashed (at home, by mom or dad) with a hammer.
- 4 tablespoons rock salt
- Mixing bowls
- 1 lb coffee can with plastic lid
- 3 lb coffee can with plastic lid
- Large spoon
- Measuring cups
- Towel (optional)
- Duct tape (optional)

1. Measure and pour milk, cream, sugar and flavoring into a mixing bowl before you start the experiment.

2. Stir these ingredients well.

3. Pour this mixture into the one-pound coffee can.

4. Place the lid securely on the can and set it inside the three-pound can.

5. Add ice and salt, in alternate layers, around the small can that is inside the larger one.

6. When the large can is full of ice and salt, secure its lid.

Mom or Dad: You may want to help your child duct-tape the lid of the larger can to prevent any ice or water from leaking out.

7. Place a sheet on the floor or wrap the can in a large towel.

8. Let your child roll the can back and forth on the floor for at least 10 minutes. (See "A note on timing," page 81.)

9. After 10 minutes, open the cans and check the ice cream.

10. If it is not starting to freeze, replace lids and roll for 5 more minutes. The ice cream should be frozen to the sides and bottom of the can. If it is not thick enough, place the smaller can in the freezer for ten minutes.

11. Once it is frozen, taste it. In your "ice cream journal" (see page 83) describe the taste, texture, color, and richness.

12. Start over! Now try different flavor combinations.

A NOTE ON TIMING:

Just like in the Butter Battle recipes, rolling a can for 10 minutes might get a bit tedious. Try singing your way through it. To the tune of "Row, Row, Row Your Boat," make up words or sing: "Roll, Roll, Roll your cream/Make it soft and icy. Roll it fast, and roll it slow to make an icy treat." Make up words to all your favorite songs. Or play the game "how many ice cream flavors can you name."

SUPERMARKET TUBS VS. "SOFT SERVE"

When you have a finished product, you will notice that your home-made ice cream really bears little resemblance to the hard stuff we buy at the supermarket. It is the temperature and the amount of whipping (rolling in this case) that totally change the texture. The stuff you make at home is more like "soft serve" ice cream, which is made at about 18 degrees Fahrenheit. The packaged ice cream sold in grocery stores is made at about the same temperature but "hardened" by going through a -40 degree Fahrenheit tunnel. It then remains stored at a much colder temperature so it can travel and maintain its quality. Without this trip through the "deep freeze," traditional soft serve just wouldn't stand up in the store or home freezer.

Moreover, packaged ice cream usually contains more fat globules than soft serve. The warmer temperature of soft serve allows our taste buds to detect more flavors than hard frozen packaged ice cream.

Most low-fat packaged ice cream is whipped more than the regular stuff. The whipping allows for more air in the mixture and thus gives it a smoother texture. This trick makes your tongue think it's tasting the smoothness of fat globules!

TAKE IT FURTHER:

- Compare the results to commercial ice cream. How is it different, and what would you change in the basic recipe?
- Have your child design her own recipe. She can change such things as the flavoring, the amount of sugar, or the type of liquid used in the recipe.
- Explore how the taste, texture, color, and richness change by using milks with different amounts of butterfat, including skim milk, 1 percent milk, 2 percent milk, whole milk, Half & Half, or just heavy cream.

  (**Hint**: The more butterfat a recipe has in it, the creamier the ice cream will be.)

- Explore the world of Ben & Jerry's ice cream at http://www.benjerry.com. You can take a virtual factory tour, play ice cream games, and print paper-craft projects.

ICE CREAM LARRY DATA SHEET

Ice Cream Taste Test:

	Type A Store-bought Vanilla ice cream	Type B ½ whole milk And ½ heavy cream	Type C Your recipe #1	Type D Your recipe #2
Describe the color.				
Does it have a vanilla smell?				
Describe ice cream's texture: Smooth, bumpy, shiny, etc.?				
Does it taste sweet?				
Can you feel the ice crystals in the mixture?				
Overall rating: 1- Excellent, 2 – Good, 3- O.K. or 4 – Bad (or color or draw your own rating system with crayons)				

83

NOTES:

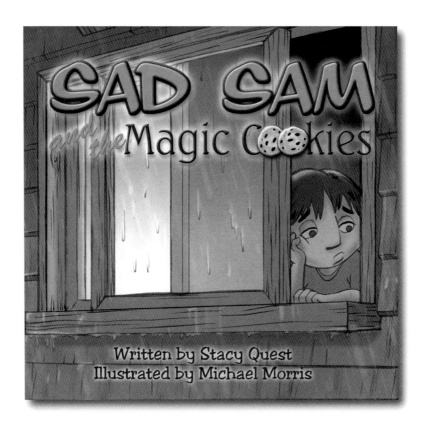

CHAPTER 9

Sad Sam and
the Magic Cookies

By Stacey Quest.
Michael Morris, illustrator.
BookBound Publishing, Los Angeles: 2007.

Other good reads: *Cookie Magic* by Geraldine Mabin and
Lynn Seligman; *Twelve Plump Cookies* by Larry Dane Brimner;
My Mom by Anthony Browne

THE STORY:

Most kids can relate to poor Sam! It's cold and rainy, and he's stuck inside with nothing to do. Maxi the dog won't play with him. And he can't even manage to make meatball sauce without knocking the bowl off the counter and then slipping in the mess! Fortunately, Mom has a magic cookie recipe — and an even more important magic cookie rule — to cheer him up.

Sam's story is the perfect opener for an exploration into the magical science of baking cookies. Have your kids experiment with cookie batches by changing ingredients here and there and keeping track of the results. Which cookies are more crumbly and which are thicker? Along the way, they'll discover how the magic cookie rule mixed with some scientific know-how can take away the blues.

● ●

THE SCIENCE OF MAGIC COOKIES:

Bake'em soft & chewy or hard & crumbly

According to the Home Baking Association, the average American consumes about 300 cookies a year. But have you ever really considered the science behind those cookies?

In this experiment, you will bake multiple batches of Snickerdoodle cookies to compare texture and see how the type of fat used affects the cookie's "spreadability." This simple recipe is ideal for our experiment because it can be altered easily to change the texture of the cookie from soft and chewy to hard and crumbly.

Before getting started making cookies as a scientific experiment, you'll need some basic scientific and chemical facts about their ingredients.

Flour is the main ingredient of any type of cookie and provides its structure. The gluten — or protein — in flour forms a netting that traps air bubbles. Its starch meanwhile helps the cookie to set as it heats, which builds and bolsters its structure. The kind of flour used in cookie-making is soft and lower in protein than, for example, cake flour or all-purpose flour. Make sure to use the proper flour and to measure carefully. Even one extra teaspoon of flour will make a big difference in how a cookie spreads and rises.

Sugar is the next most important ingredient found in all types of cookies. Not only does it add sweetness, but it also has a scientific purpose in the recipe. When you cream sugar and fat together at the start of the recipe, you are trapping air in this mixture, thereby creating a more tender cookie consistency. The sugar blocks the formation of gluten in the dough as it bakes.

Leavening agents allow your cookies to rise. As the carbon dioxide forms, it is trapped by the gluten and starch in the dough as it bakes. Cream of tartar, baking powder and baking soda are the main leaveners used in cookie dough. Note that these three are not interchangeable. Baking soda and cream of tartar are acidic and relax the gluten in the cookie dough, helping the cookie to spread. Baking powder, on the other hand, contains both an acid and soda (a base). The combination of acid and base means leavening will occur while mixing the dough and again while baking it. Cookies with baking powder will spread less. (See "Baking Powder vs. Baking Soda" sidebar [page 88]).

Eggs also act as a leavening agent by adding steam to the mixture as it bakes. The yolk of an egg adds fat for a tender and light texture. The yolk also acts as an emulsifier for a smooth and even texture during baking. In all cookie recipes you must use large eggs, but you can decrease the number of eggs you use by substituting water, vanilla, or milk. Those products will tend to make the cookie spread out because they are liquids.

Butter, shortening, vegetable oil, and margarine are all forms of fats found in cookie recipes. The fats add rich flavor and a creamy texture. When you combine fat, especially butter, with sugars while you're making cookie dough, tiny air pockets form. These pockets fill with carbon dioxide gas from the leaveners as the cookies bake.

The type of fat you use in a recipe will also affect how much a cookie spreads. Butter and margarine are 80 percent fat and 20 percent liquid. The liquid in margarine is water, and the liquid in butter is buttermilk. Shortening and vegetable oil are 100 percent fat and contain no liquids. Vegetable or cooking oil does not hold air and, therefore, will not cream with sugar. Some types of cookies will then be greasy and too thin when baked with oil and shortening. Shortening and margarine are hydrogenated fats. They will melt more slowly than butter in baking, and the resulting cookie may be thicker and chewier than the others.

Baking Soda vs. Baking Powder: What is the difference?

Have you ever wondered what would happen if you swapped one white powdery leavener for the other? Here's a rundown of how these two vital kitchen ingredients work.

Baking soda, which is also used as an antacid, a deodorizer for the refrigerator, and a scouring cleanser, is mainly used in quick-cooking recipes. Made of sodium bicarbonate, which is a base (see the ABCs of Acids and Bases, p. 31), baking soda must be mixed with an acidic ingredient in order to become a leavener. Buttermilk, fruit juice, applesauce, sour cream, honey, chocolate, and yogurt are all acidic ingredients that work. During the baking process, the acid-base reaction causes carbon dioxide bubbles to form inside the dough, making the cookies rise. Baking soda is unstable at high temperatures for long periods of time, which is why it is most used for quick-cooking goodies such as cookies or pancakes. Also, dough that contains baking soda and acid must be cooked quickly after they're mixed together since the leavener works during the mixing phase. Using baking soda alone in a recipe without an acidifying ingredient will cause the cookies to taste bitter and prevent them from rising.

Baking powder, on the other hand, is best for recipes that require high heat for long periods of time like cakes, cupcakes, breads, and muffins. Since baking powder contains both an acid and a base, some rising will occur during the mixing phase. However, most of the carbon dioxide gas will be produced during the baking. Baking powder has no effect on the taste of the cookie, since the acid and base neutralize during the mixing and baking.

HYDROGENATED FATS AND TRANS-FATS

Hydrogenated fats — those found in margarine and shortening — are created in labs through a process called hydrogenation. During this process, hydrogen and metal catalysts are added to plant-based, unsaturated fats like corn oil. Processing causes the liquid fat to stiffen and start to solidify at room temperature. This gives the fat a longer shelf life than butter. Moreover, the hydrogenated fats mimic the texture of butter and lard for a much cheaper price.

As a result of this chemical process, unsaturated fat becomes more saturated and contains trans-fatty acids, which are synthetic saturated fats. These trans-fatty acids, while mimicking the texture and at times the taste of butter and lard, are difficult for the body to digest. They raise a person's LDL levels, the bad cholesterol, while lowering one's HDL levels, good cholesterol.

Additionally, these fats interfere with the metabolic absorption of food, are a poor source of energy for the body, and are difficult to excrete from the body. Studies have shown an association between the consumption of trans-fatty acids and heart disease.

89

NOT A CANDY BAR

The Snickerdoodle cookie — a sugar cookie rolled in cinnamon and nutmeg — is fundamentally a mini-cake containing fewer sources of liquid ingredients (milk, eggs, water, etc.) than a cake. This cookie originated with Dutch and German settlers of the New England states during the early nineteenth century. However, evidence suggests that the ancient Romans baked a similar type of cookie. Feel free to add chocolate chips, nuts, or dried fruit to the recipe when you're done with the experiment.

THE EXPERIMENT **& what you'll need:**

For basic cookie dough (makes 2 dozen cookies)

- 1 ¼ cups and 2 tablespoons (1/8 c.) all-purpose flour
- ¾ cup granulated sugar
- ½ cup butter - softened
- 1 large egg
- 1 teaspoon cream of tartar
- ½ teaspoon baking soda
- ½ teaspoon vanilla
- ⅛ teaspoon salt
- Large mixing bowl
- Mixing spoons
- Measuring spoons and cups
- Electric mixer (optional)

For cookie coating
- 2 tablespoons sugar
- ½ teaspoon cinnamon
- ½ teaspoon nutmeg
- Small bowl or pan
- Fork
- Cookie pan
- Oven timer or stopwatch (optional)
- Ruler

1. Preheat oven to 400 degrees Fahrenheit.

2. In a large mixing bowl, combine the flour, sugar, butter, egg, cream of tartar, baking soda, vanilla and salt.

3. Blend all ingredients until well mixed. You may do it by hand or on the low-speed setting of your mixer. Make sure to scrape the sides of the mixing bowl.

4. Roll out one-inch balls of dough with a spoon, taking care to make them as close as possible in size. Set aside.

5. In a small bowl or pan, mix sugar, cinnamon and nutmeg with a fork.

6. Roll each ball of dough in this sugar and spice mixture.

7. Place each dough ball on an ungreased cookie pan approximately two inches apart.

8. In the preheated oven, bake the dough for 9 minutes until it turns golden brown.

9. Track how long it takes the largest ball of dough to flatten out into a cookie. Write it down on your data chart.

10. Allow the cookies to cool before you observe and taste them.

11. Select the largest cookie of the batch and measure its width. Describe the flavor and texture (crumby, smooth, greasy or coarse) of the cookie. Write everything down on your data sheet.

12. Repeat steps #1 – 11 changing the types of fat used in the recipe. These variations can be:

   - ½ cup of shortening instead of butter
   - ½ cup of vegetable oil instead of butter
   - ½ cup of margarine instead of butter
   - ¼ cup butter and ¼ cup shortening

13. Compare all data and decide which type of fat created the best Snickerdoodle cookie.

COUNT YOUR CHIPS

Munch your way through math using chocolate chip or M&M candy cookies as your manipulatives. As you and your child munch through a batch, keep a tally of the number of chips or M&M candies that are eaten in a cookie. Compare your totals to observe if chips or M&Ms are equally spread throughout a batch of cookies.

TAKE IT FURTHER:

- Share your cookies! Give family members and friends separate bags, each containing a Snickerdoodle from the different batches. Have them compare cookies and vote on their favorite. You can keep track of people's preferences and create a pictograph of the data (using cookies as the pictures).
- Sad Sam's cookies were "magical." Allow your child to develop her own magic cookie rules and recipe. Allow her to add nuts, chocolate chips, sprinkles, dried fruit, or icing to the basic recipe.
- Cookie painting! Flatten out the balls of Snickerdoodle dough and do not coat it with the sugar and spice mixture. Mix 1 egg yolk with six drops of food coloring. Beat well using a whisk or a fork. Using a clean paint brush, have your child paint images on the flattened surface of the dough. Bake the cookies according to the recipe, but allow them to sit in the baking pan to cool for two minutes before removing them. You can use many yolks to make different colors for your chef Picasso or patissier (pastry chef) Monet.

SAD SAM AND THE MAGIC COOKIES DATA SHEET

How does the type of fat you use change a cookie?

	Butter	½ Cup Shortening	½ Cup Vegetable Oil	½ Cup Margarine	¼ Cup and ¼ Cup Shortening
Cookie Spread (width of the cookie)					
Cookie Flavor (sweet, tangy, bland, etc.)					
Cookie Texture (crumby, smooth, greasy, etc.)					
Cookie Rating 1= Awful, 2= Not good, 3= O.K., 4= Good, 5= Fantastic					

NOTES:

CHAPTER 10
Everybody Bakes Bread

By Norah Dooley.
Peter J. Thornton, illustrator.
Lerner Publishing Group, Minneapolis, MN: 1996.

Other good reads: *Bread Is for Eating* by David and Phyllis
Gershator; *Tony's Bread* by Tomie de Paola;
Loaves of Fun: A History of Bread by Elizabeth M. Harbison

THE STORY:

If your kids have ever gone stir-crazy in the kitchen while you baked treats, they'll understand why this book's heroine excitedly sets out in the rain to find a neighbor who can loan her mother a "three-handled rolling pin." Carrie knocks on door after door in her culturally diverse neighborhood. But instead of finding this elusive object, she ends up on a gastronomical journey. Each door introduces Carrie's palate to bread from a different culture: From sweet Southern cornbread to El Salvadorian pupusas, and from Indian chapatis to Barbadian coconut bread. The final section of *Everybody Bakes Bread* contains recipes for each type of bread Carrie samples on her quest.

This book will provide an inspiration next time you've got a rainy day and some yeast and flour in the pantry. After you've baked one of the several bread recipes in the book, this experiment will show you how yeast, a key ingredient, works.

●●●●●●●●●●●●●●●●●●●●●●●●●●●●●●●●●●●●●●

96

THE SCIENCE:

Learn what makes dough rise!

Yeast, as most of us know, is a crucial ingredient in bread-making. But it is more than just a powder in a packet. It also is a one-celled, living fungus that can both make bread rise and help beer ferment. This tiny plant-like microorganism exists all around us in the soil, on plants and even in the air. The word yeast comes from the Old English "gist," meaning bubble or foam. There are several hundred species of yeast, but one type, *Saccharomyces cerivisiae,* has been used in baking since ancient Egyptian times — about 4,000 years ago.

The goal of a yeast cell is to digest a food source in order to grow. Yeast's favorite food is sugar. It likes sucrose, which comes from cane sugar and sugar beets; it devours fructose and glucose, from honey, molasses, and fruit; and it also enjoys maltose, which originates in the starch found in flour.

In 1857, the French biologist and chemist Louis Pasteur discovered that yeast breaks down or decomposes the sugars in flour and then produces carbon dioxide gas. As the carbon dioxide bubbles are produced, the gluten proteins in the flour expand, causing bread dough to rise.

💡 **Hint:** Although it's hard to see a microorganism without a microscope, in this experiment, you will be able to see evidence of yeast living and working inside plastic baggies with different amounts of sugar added. The bubbles inside are evidence that the yeast is alive and eating. The more sugar you have in a bag, the more carbon dioxide is being produced, which in turn means breaking down of complex sugars inside the bag. The yeast in the bag marked "0" contains no sugar for the yeast to "eat", so no carbon dioxide. Hence, there are no bubbles and the bag won't expand.

The idea is to look for the bag that rises or expands the most. It should be the one with the most sugar, since that would produce the most carbon dioxide. In simple terms, the more sugar there is in the dough, the higher it will rise.

THE EXPERIMENT & what you'll need:

- 4 quart-size Ziploc bags
- 4 packets of activated dry yeast
- 2 teaspoons sugar
- 6 cups warm water (about 46 degrees Celsius or 115 degrees Fahrenheit)
- Large bowl
- Permanent marker
- Thermometer
- Piece of cardboard (or notebook with a stiff back)
- Ruler

1. Pour one packet of activated dry yeast into each Ziploc bag.

2. Add 1 teaspoon of sugar to one bag and label it "1 tsp."

3. Add ½ teaspoon of sugar to another bag and label it "½ tsp."

4. Add ¼ teaspoon of sugar to the fourth bag and label it "¼ tsp."

5. Mark "0" on the outside of the last bag and do not add any sugar to it. This bag will be your control.

6. Pour warm water into the large bowl so it is about ⅔ full. Check the temperature of the water with the thermometer. The water should be about 46 degrees Celsius or 115 degrees Fahrenheit. You may need to add hot or cold water to bring the water to the correct temperature.

7. Use the measuring cup to dip ¼ cup of warm water from the bowl into each of the bags.

8. Squeeze most of the air out of the bags and seal them.

9. Gently squeeze each bag between your fingers to mix the contents thoroughly. Make sure that there are no dry pockets of yeast or sugar in the bags.

10. Set the bags in the bowl of warm water in a warm place so they will not cool down rapidly. Leave them for 30 to 40 minutes.

11. Take the bag marked "0" out of the water, dry it, and place it on a flat table. You should then put the cardboard or notebook on top of the bag, holding the table level. Use the ruler to measure the distance from the table to the bottom of the cardboard.

12. Record your measurements on your data sheet.

13. Repeat step 11 with the remaining bags.

TALKING IT OVER:

Here are some questions to get your child thinking about the experiment:

Can you tell which bag contained the most carbon dioxide gas? How do you know this?

Why do you think this bag has more carbon dioxide gas than the others?

What do you think would happen if you repeated this experiment with 2 tsp of sugar in the bag? Try it and see!

Connecting science with fiction:

Explore the role bread plays in your family's life. Call a grandparent, aunt, uncle or cousin to find your family's bread recipes (bread, biscuits, rolls, etc.) Your child can ask the family member to recount anecdotes about the family's "baker" or give a history of the recipe. If the stories are interesting, turn them into an oral history, type it up and use old photos and bread recipes. A family baking book would make a fun holiday or birthday gift — along with a smattering of family bread and baked goods.

TAKE IT FURTHER:

Explore the world of gluten, take a microscopic tour of bread, and explore more cultures and their breads at: http://www.exploratorium.edu/cooking/bread/index.html

Try this great experiment to show your child how yeast acts as a decomposer!

1. Cut two slices from a banana, each approximately 2 centimeters long.

2. Place each slice in its own Ziploc bag.

3. Add approximately ½ tsp. of yeast on top of ONE of the bananas. Make sure the yeast lands on the surface of the banana.

4. Seal both bags and label each bag with the date and description of what is in the bag.

5. Record an observation for this first day in a notebook. Make sure to describe carefully each bag's contents.

6. Each day for the next three to four days observe the two bags and record all observations in your notebook. Do not open the bags during this phase.

7. At the end of the fifth day, your child will see how the yeast has eaten sections of the banana. Also, carbon dioxide bubbles should form on the surface of thebanana.

8. Throw the bags away upon the conclusion of the experiment.

• •

EVERYBODY BAKES BREAD
ORAL HISTORY ACTIVITY

A History of Our Family's Bread

Our family's bread maker is/was _____.

How is he or she related to me? _____

When and where was this person born?
_____

What do you remember most about the bread that
_____ baked? Why was it so memorable?
_____

_____

Was this bread baked for special occasions or was it part of
the family's daily meals?   101
_____

_____

This is our family's bread recipe:

This is a picture of our family's bread baker:

EVERYBODY BAKES BREAD DATA SHEET

Measure the thickness of the yeast bags to compare how much carbon dioxide is being produced inside each one. Write your outcomes on the data sheet. You can also draw pictures of the bags with their different reactions.

Amount of carbon dioxide in the bag (measured in centimeters)

Bag with "0" sugar	
Bag with "¼ tsp" sugar	
Bag with " ½ tsp" sugar	
Bag with "1 tsp" sugar	

103

NOTES:

104

CHAPTER 11
How to Make an Apple Pie and See the World

By Marjorie Priceman.
Alfred A. Knopf, 1994.

Other good reads: *Apples* by Jacqueline Farmer and Phyllis Limbacher Tildes; *The President and Mom's Apple Pie* by Michael Garland

THE STORY:

How do you make an apple pie when the market is closed? According to this colorful book, you can try crisscrossing the globe to gather your ingredients: semolina wheat from Italy, elegant eggs (and a hen) from France, sugar cane from Jamaica, and of course delectable apples from Vermont. Along the way, your child will learn that food comes from farther away than the grocery store, and that it must be harvested, milled, cooked, churned, and then travel before it can become a tasty treat.

The book includes an easy recipe for "real" apple pie from scratch, which your child may want to try. Go for it! You can also use the book to introduce the idea of baking an apple pie the artificial way — without apples!

. . . .

THE SCIENCE:

Make a fake apple pie with fun flavorings!

Some historians believe that the recipe for mock apple pie originated during the Civil War and was created by soldiers hungry for a taste of home. While we may never know the true origin of this recipe, mock apple pie, also known as "soda cracker pie," has been used as a cheap alternative to using real apples. The real magic in this recipe comes from a chemical reaction caused by the cream of tartar you will use.

Apples contain tartaric acid and malic acid, which give them their distinctive fresh, slightly tart taste. By adding cream of tartar, an acidic compound closely related to tartaric acid, to the other ingredients, you are helping the crackers hold their shape. Cream of tartar also prevents the sugar syrup from crystallizing during the baking. It breaks down the sucrose in the sugar syrup into glucose and fructose, and results in a sugary concoction that approximates the sweetness of apples. The texture and masking of flavors trick your brain into thinking you are eating real apples.

Cream of tartar, known also as potassium hydrogen tartrate, is a by-product of winemaking. Essentially, cream of tartar is a salt that forms inside wine barrels in the form of crystals as wine ages. The salt crystals are removed and packaged as cream of tartar, a helpful addition to your pantry. The acids within the cream of tartar will keep fruits and vegetables from browning (or oxidizing) after being cut. It will also keep sugars from crystallizing, thus giving whipped egg whites, candies, and creams a smooth texture.

THE EXPERIMENT & what you'll need:

- Pie pastry for a two-crust 9-inch pie or two ready-made pie crusts
- 36 Ritz Crackers, coarsely broken (about 1 ¾ cups crumbs)
- 1 ¾ cups water
- 2 cups sugar
- 2 teaspoons cream of tartar
- 2 tablespoons lemon juice
- Grated peel of one lemon
- 2 tablespoons of butter
- ½ teaspoon ground cinnamon

107

1. Preheat oven to 425 degrees Fahrenheit.

2. Roll out the bottom half of the pastry to line a 9-inch pie plate. This step is not necessary if you're using a pre-made pie crust that's already in a foil baking tin.

3. Place cracker crumbs in the prepared crust; set aside.

4. Heat water, sugar, and cream of tartar to a boil in saucepan over high heat; simmer for 15 minutes.

5. Add lemon juice and lemon peel and stir. Allow the syrup to cool.

6. Pour the cooled syrup over the cracker crumbs.

7. Dot with butter and sprinkle with cinnamon.

8. Roll out remaining pastry, and place it over the pie.

9. Trim, seal and flute edges.

10. Slit top crust to allow steam to escape.

11. Bake for 30 to 35 minutes or until crust is crisp and golden.

12. Set aside and allow the pie to cool completely.

13. Follow the "real" apple pie recipe at the end of *How to Make an Apple Pie and See the World*, or go to the grocery store and purchase a real apple pie.

14. Compare the two pies and write down your findings on your data sheet.

CONNECTING SCIENCE WITH FICTION:

Using a world map, follow step-by-step the baker's itinerary as you gather her ingredients to make the apple pie.

Research each place visited on the baker's journey online. Then create a travel brochure or postcard to represent the different countries and states. Place the brochures or postcards in a collage for display.

Go on a "food safari" through the grocery store to map out the origins of your food. You can note the results on your world map (see activity above).

TAKE IT FURTHER:

- Create apple stamps using any real apples left over from pie-baking. Cut an apple in half horizontally instead of vertically. This reveals the star center where the apple seeds grow. Dip one half of the apple in paint and have your child stamp the star center on construction paper, wooden picture frames or fabric. Use different sizes and varieties of apples to create different patterns. Crab apples work well.

- Conduct a blind taste test among family members to see if they can tell the difference between "real" apple pie and "mock" apple pie. Create a pictograph of their responses. Use your apple stamps as the symbols on the graph.

- Teach your child about a map's key and scale! Take out a world map and help her determine how many miles the baker traveled on her journey to collect the ingredients. Then have your child plot a shorter route for the baker to take the next time she makes a pie. Have them use their cardinal directions (North, South, East and West on the compass rose) and intermediate directions (NE, NW, SE and SW) in a letter to the baker.

109

HOW TO MAKE AN APPLE PIE AND
SEE THE WORLD DATA SHEET

Check off the characteristic that best describes each pie.

	Real apple pie	**Mock apple pie**
Sweetness	Very sweet _____ Sweet_____ Not sweet _____	Very sweet _____ Sweet _____ Not sweet _____
Taste of apples	Apple taste _____ No apple taste _____	Apple taste _____ No apple taste
Appearance of pie	Looks like apples _____ Does not look like apples _____	Looks like apples_____ Does not look like apples _____
Crispness of apples	Very crisp_____ Not very crisp _____	Very crisp _____ Not very crisp _____
Overall opinion of pie	Likes _____ Needs improvement _____ Dislike _____	Likes _____ Needs improvement _____ Dislike_____

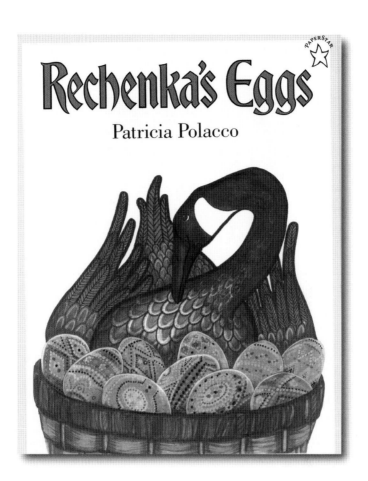

CHAPTER 12
Rechenka's Eggs

By Patricia Polacco.
Penguin Putnam, New York: 1988.

Other good reads: *Henri, Egg Artiste* by Marcus Pfister;
*Berry Smudges and Leaf Prints: Finding and
Making Colors from Nature* by Ellen B. Senisi

THE STORY:

Kids love painting Easter eggs, and this enchanting tale of Babushka and her intricately painted eggs is sure to inspire their imaginations. Babushka is a small, stout Russian woman, modeled on Polacco's grandmother. Each winter Babushka prepares her beautifully painted eggs for the Easter Festival in Moscow. One day, she finds an injured goose, takes her in, and names her Rechenka, which means miracle. Each morning, the thankful goose lays an egg that Babushka can intricately paint.

In a sad turn of events that nearly breaks Babushka's heart and prevents her from attending the festival, Rechenka manages to break the adorned eggs. But true to her name, the next day some intricately painted eggs arrive nonetheless! Whether or not you celebrate Easter, you can use this lovely tale to introduce your child to egg artistry and teach him about the science behind dyeing eggs, using weak acid and natural dyes.

· ·

THE SCIENCE:

Dye eggs & create art using natural ingredients!

The main ingredient of eggshells is calcium carbonate. This is the same brittle material found in teeth, chalk, sea shells, coral, and limestone (for more on the anatomy of eggshells, see the chapter on *Daisy and the Egg*, p. 149). Calcium carbonate is also alkali, which means it is a base (for more on acids and bases, see "The ABCs of Acids and Bases" on p. 31, as well as the activity for *George's Marvelous Medicine* by Roald Dahl, p. 37).

When you place boiled eggs in vinegar and water, the vinegar starts the chemical reaction. The vinegar is an acid, and it breaks down the smooth layer of the outer shell (a base). The acid makes it easier for the dye to seep into the pores of the shell and set the color. However, if you actually leave an egg in vinegar too long, the reaction between the calcium carbonate and the vinegar will dissolve the entire shell.

Natural Dyes

Dyes obtained from natural products, such as plants and insects, have been used for decorative effects and as symbols of status for thousands of years. Egg dyes used in this experiment are natural dyes that can be made from everyday foods. They include blue from cabbage leaves or blueberries, orange from yellow onion skins, red from cranberries or raspberries, pale green from spinach leaves, and light yellow from orange or lemon peels. Dyes often have different colors in acidic and alkaline (or base) solutions. This enables some plants to be used as acid-base indicators.

Below is a listing of natural materials you can use to dye the eggs and the colors they will produce.

Natural material	Color produced
Yellow onion	Orange to brown
Beet juice	Bright pink
Grape juice	Purple to lavender
Purple cabbage	Bluish-purple
Cranberry juice	Light pink
Spinach (fresh)	Yellow-green
Blueberries	Bluish
Coffee	Caramel brown
Orange and lemon peels	Yellow
Red onion	Magenta

THE EXPERIMENT & what you'll need:

- A dozen eggs (or more)
- 1 glass or stainless steel bowl per dye you intend to make
- 1 teaspoon of white vinegar per color
- Spoons, preferably wooden
- Metric measuring cups
- Aprons and paper towels
- Cooking oil (optional)

Natural materials for dyeing:
- skin of one yellow onion
- skin of one red onion
- 1 head purple cabbage
- 1 cup beet juice
- 1 cup grape juice
- 1 cup cranberry juice
- 1 cup fresh spinach
- 1 cup blueberries
- 1 cup brewed coffee
- 1 cup orange or lemon peel

1. Gently place a single layer of eggs in a large sauce pan. Do not stack eggs on top of each other.

2. Fill the pan with tap water. Make sure the water level is ½ inch over the top of the eggs.

3. Measure two teaspoons of white vinegar and add the vinegar to the sauce pan.

4. Observe the eggs. Do you see any changes? Do you see small bubbles forming around the surface of the eggs? This is the vinegar reacting with the calcium carbonate in each egg's shell.

5. Add one cup of your natural dye material to the vinegar and water solution. You can add an additional cup of natural materials for a deeper and more intense color.

6. Place saucepan on the stove at medium heat.

7. Bring the water to a boil, reduce the heat to a low setting, and allow the eggs to simmer for 20 minutes.

8. Remove the pan from the heat and allow the eggs to sit in the dye solution for one hour.

9. With a strainer or slotted spoon (to pick up the eggs only, not the dye material) remove the eggs and place them in a bowl covered with a paper towel. Keep the strained liquid.

10. If the coloring is too light, you can put the eggs back in the dye solution and allow them to soak overnight, but no longer than 8 hours.

11. Be careful...the vinegar will weaken the egg shells if you leave them overnight.

12. Dry the eggs by placing them on a paper towel.

13. To give the eggs a high-gloss appearance, you can rub cooking oil over the surface of the colored eggshell.

A NOTE ABOUT MAKING NATURAL DYES:

If you want to make several dyes separately so you'll have many on hand at once, as opposed to doing one pot at a time as described above, follow this simple recipe.

Use about two cups of water, one cup or more of dye materials and a teaspoon of white vinegar for each egg you plan to dye in the finished color.

Mix the water, vinegar and materials in a large pot and bring it to a quick boil, stirring frequently with a wooden spoon.

As soon as it reaches a boil, reduce heat immediately to medium-low, and let simmer very gently for at least 25 minutes and no more than 45 minutes.

Keep each dye in a container with a lid. Be sure to label each one until you use it.

TAKE IT FURTHER:

- Learn about the history and process of making beautiful Ukrainian Easter eggs like Babushka's. You may even try your hand at it. Check out: http://www.learnpysanky.com/ or http://go.hrw.com/hrw.nd/gohrw_rls1/pKeywordResults?sg1%20pysansky%2018
- Explore the world of Faberge and his brilliantly decorated eggs with your child at PBS's Treasures of the World site: http://www.pbs.org/treasuresoftheworld/a_nav/faberge_nav/main_fabfrm.html
- Try other substances you find at home, like flower petals, soda, leaves, and other vegetables, to create other natural dye solutions. Record your findings in a journal, so you can recreate the colors.
- Check out http://www.patriciapolacco.com/index.htm to learn more about Rechenka's creator and to try a Rechenka-related quiz.

CONNECTING SCIENCE WITH FICTION:

Here are a few questions to start a conversation about Babushka and her eggs:

What kind of person is Babushka? Can you think of some adjectives to describe her? What in the book makes you describe her as you do? Do you know anyone like Babushka?

From the pictures, can you tell which natural dyes she would want to use if she didn't have paint? What do you think Rechenka has inside to be able to lay such colorful eggs?

What is Rechenka's final miracle?

SCIENTIST'S NOTEBOOK FOR *RECHENKA'S EGGS*

Use this space to test colors, draw and design eggs and take notes!

NOTES:

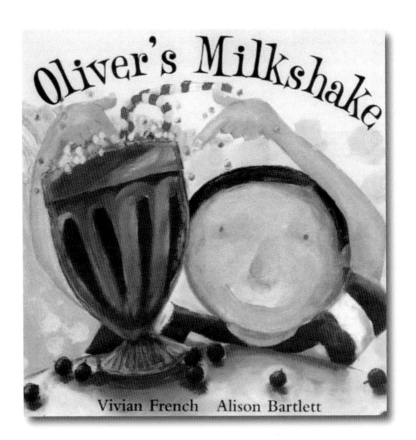

Vivian French   Alison Bartlett

C H A P T E R   1 3
Oliver's Milkshake

By Vivian French.
Alison Bartlett, illustrator.
Hodder Children's Books, UK: 2001.

THE STORY:

If your child is particular about what she eats, then she will have great sympathy for Oliver, the quintessential picky eater. In this brightly colored picture book, Oliver feels finicky about milk. His mom frets when she sees him drinking orange soda for breakfast (good grief!). But then he goes on a "shopping" trip with his Aunt Jen where the fresh milk comes from cows and the fruit comes from trees and bushes... it's a farm! As they gather blueberries and milk to make a "yummy scrummy fruity frothy icy nicy dreamy creamy" shake, Oliver reconsiders his milk aversion.

Oliver's Milk Shake will remind your child that milk does not come from the grocery store but from nature. Use it to start a conversation about the different kinds of milk we drink and what their differences mean. Your child can then grab a straw and (oh, no!) blow bubbles in his milk to see how its fat content affects the bubbles. This could be a frothy situation!

Connecting Science with Fiction:

After you've finished with the bubbles experiment, gather the ingredients Oliver and Aunt Jen assembled to make your own smoothie-shake in the blender. Then experiment with other fruits such as peaches, mangoes, strawberries, and pineapple, and conduct a taste test.

 Hint: If you can't go to a local farm for the freshest milk and berries, then regular milk and store-bought fruit will do. If you use frozen fruit, you can leave out the ice and intensify the flavor!

NOTE: Your child may squeal with "udder" delight when he finds out he gets to blow bubbles in his beverage. However, it could turn into a kitchen disaster. Give him the responsibility of developing rules for this experiment so your kitchen does not turn into a foamy mess.

THE SCIENCE:

Blow bubbles in milk & measure the foam

We're all familiar with the different types of milk — whole, two percent, one percent, skim, and buttermilk. The milk carton's label indicates the amount of milk fat found inside. When raw milk comes from a cow, it contains about four percent milk fat. This milk fat comes in the form of cream. As milk is processed, different amounts of cream are "skimmed" out of the beverage with skim milk containing less than one percent milk fat.

Whole milk is basically raw milk that has been processed, meaning that it has been both pasteurized and homogenized. If you left whole milk out on the counter (without refrigeration) for a while, a cream layer would form on the top. The cream is made up of the fat globules floating in milk. They rise and form a cream layer while the milk below will be a partially "skim" milk, since most of the fat globules are sitting at the surface. Most consumers would find this separating of milk parts unappealing, so the dairy industry processes, or homogenizes, the milk.

To do that, the milk must pass through a high-pressure system in which the fat droplets squeeze through wire screens that break the globules into much smaller droplets. Their surfaces become coated with protein, and the fat blends together with the liquid, making the globules more stable and less likely to form the cream layer. However, if you let milk sit in your refrigerator long enough, a cream layer will form at the same time that the milk starts to spoil.

121

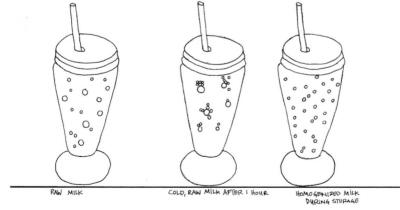

Fat globules in different types of milk.

WHY DOES SKIM MAKE BETTER CAPPUCCINO?

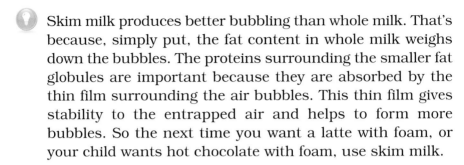

Skim milk produces better bubbling than whole milk. That's because, simply put, the fat content in whole milk weighs down the bubbles. The proteins surrounding the smaller fat globules are important because they are absorbed by the thin film surrounding the air bubbles. This thin film gives stability to the entrapped air and helps to form more bubbles. So the next time you want a latte with foam, or your child wants hot chocolate with foam, use skim milk.

Before you begin

Review with your child some of the facts he learned making butter in *The Butter Battle Book* chapter. Remind him that milk contains milk fat, and that skim milk contains less milk fat than whole milk. Tell your child to start thinking about how milk fat might affect how many bubbles he can make in the milk with a straw. Have him make up a hypothesis and write it down on his data sheet.

THE EXPERIMENT & what you'll need:

- ½ cup whole milk
- ½ cup skim milk
- Two 8-oz. clear plastic cups
- Non-bendable straws
- Stopwatch
- Marking pen

1. Label one cup "whole" and the other "skim" with your marking pen.

2. Add ½ cup of cold whole milk to the "whole" cup and set aside.

3. Add ½ cup of cold skim milk to the "skim" cup and set aside.

4. Place a non-bendable straw in each cup.

5. Allow cups to sit out for 20 minutes, so they reach room temperature.

6. Blow simultaneously into both straws for one minute. Use the stop watch for an exact measurement of time.

7. Measure the height of the bubble column that forms inside each cup. You are measuring the volume of the foam. Now record the measurement on your data sheet.

8. Switch the two cups' positions, so if the skim started on the left side, you move it to the right side, and so forth.

9. Blow simultaneously into both straws for one minute again. Make sure your child is blowing the same amount and strength of air into the cups.

10. Measure the height of the bubble column that forms and record the measurement on the data sheet.

11. Compare the two columns.

12. Repeat the experiment twice more to gather enough data for a comparison of the fat's effect on bubble production. Remember, this is called a scientific trial, and you'll do it to see if the results of your experiment are consistent.

TAKE IT FURTHER:

* Develop a hypothesis and then test it! Chill ½ cups of whole and skim milk in an ice-filled pan for five minutes and repeat the experiment. Collect your data and compare these results to the original experiment's results. Does the temperature of milk affect its ability to make bubbles?

* Delve further into the temperature experiment with scalded milk and see the results. Mom or Dad: Make sure you and not your child cooks the milk. Remember, scalded

milk is extremely hot and should not be sipped by your child through the straws. It can burn his mouth!

- Milk is an excellent source of calcium, and calcium is needed for the development of healthy, strong bones. Use the "Calcium Calculator" from the Washington Dairy Council to help your child determine if he is getting enough calcium to help his growing bones. Go to http://www.eatsmart.org/external/default.asp?URL=%2Fgames%2Fc%5Fcalculator%2F

- Check out "Milk Matters," a National Institutes of Health (NIH) site for kids. http://www.nichd.nih.gov/milk/kids/kidsteens.cfm
This site is full of animated games, downloadable stories, coloring books, and puzzles. Your child can even help Bo the Bovine make his way to the Calcium Fair.

OLIVER'S MILK SHAKE DATA SHEET

Hypothesis:

Does milk fat affect how many bubbles are produced in milk? Do you think whole milk or skim milk will produce more bubbles? Why?

	Whole milk	Skim Milk
Trial #1	Height of Bubble/Foam column in _____ cm	Height of Bubble/Foam column in _____ cm
Trial #2	Height of Bubble/Foam column in _____ cm	Height of Bubble/Foam column in _____ cm
Trial #3	Height of Bubble/Foam column in _____ cm	Height of Bubble/Foam column in _____ cm
Trial #4	Height of Bubble/Foam column in _____ cm	Height of Bubble/Foam column in _____ cm

125

NOTES:

126

A MONSTER
IN MY CEREAL

Marie-Francine Hébert

CHAPTER 14
A Monster in My Cereal

By Marie-Francine Hebert.
Philippe Germain, illustrator.
Second Story Press, Toronto, 1990.

Other good reads: *How It Happens at the Cereal Company*
by Megan Rocker; *There Are Monsters Everywhere*
by Mercer Mayer (for younger readers)

THE STORY:

Kids with siblings can probably sympathize with Poppy, whose mom is (callously) accompanying her (attention-nabbing) kid brother to the hospital to have his tonsils out. That means Poppy has to stay home with Dad, and all Dad knows how to do is make dumb jokes and change the channel on the TV to his programs. The plot thickens when the monster on Poppy's cereal box winks at her and steps out to give her a hug. Could he be real? Poppy confides in him about her dad's annoying habits ... and not too soon afterwards, things around the house start to change, mysteriously, perhaps more than Poppy wants them to!

This story can help you introduce the idea of fortified cereals and what might be lurking inside. The experiment involves separating the tiny iron bits added for nutritional purposes from the cereal — kind of like finding the iron monster, who lives inside.

THE SCIENCE:

Find the magnetic monster within!

As you may know, iron is a semi-metallic, semi-strong metal. Iron is rarely found in its pure form since it oxidizes so quickly. As you'll see in this experiment, iron is also magnetic. Iron can be mined from the earth and is used in the creation of steel. Iron can oxidize, or rust, and we can recognize rusting iron by its distinctive red-orange coloring. And most nutrition-conscious moms know that iron is an essential nutrient that our bodies need in order to function properly.

Moreover, iron is also the most abundant element found in the human body. It is found in blood cells that transport oxygen known as the hemoglobin and myoglobin. It is necessary for the formation of healthy red blood cells and proper brain function. Without iron in our bloodstreams, we would become anemic, experiencing fatigue and confusion, and we'd be less able to fight off infections.

That is why food manufacturers have added fortified iron to breakfast cereals. This iron, called elemental iron, is added to food in the form of tiny metal flakes. These flakes cannot be absorbed by the body until they are oxidized in the stomach by the stomach acid, made of HCl or hydrochloric acid. After it is oxidized, the iron can be absorbed into the bloodstream for proper usage. Elemental iron does not affect the taste of the cereal or its shelf life.

THE EXPERIMENT & what you'll need:

- 1 gallon size Ziploc plastic baggie
- 1 cup iron-fortified breakfast cereal like Total or Shredded Mini-Wheats (look for any cereal containing 100 percent of iron in the nutrition labeling on the side of the box).
- Measuring cup
- Paper towels
- Hot tap water
- Very strong magnet (preferably a cow magnet, available from feed supply, veterinary and scientific supply sources)
- Blender (optional)

1. Pour the cup of cereal inside the plastic bag.

2. Using a spoon or your hands, crush the cereal into small, fine pieces. It is worth spending a lot of time on this stage — the finer and smaller the pieces, the better this experiment will work.

3. Add one cup of hot tap water to the bag and seal it.

4. Shake the bag ten times, making sure the water and cereal mix well.

5. Leave the mixture for 30 minutes and enjoy a bowl of cereal while you wait.

6. After the 30 minutes, gently tilt the bag forward so that the cereal collects on one side, and place the magnet along the outside of the bag near the cereal.

7. Run the magnet over the bottom of the bag. The iron is heavier than the slurry you have created and will sink toward the bottom of the bag.

8. Lay the bag flat on the table and stroke it with the magnet towards one corner.

9. You will observe black fuzz collecting around the surface of the magnet. This black fuzz is elemental iron that you have removed from the cereal.

NOTE: If you prefer a quicker method of unleashing the iron monster from the cereal, pour the crushed cereal and hot water into a blender. Wait 15 minutes and blend well. As the slurry blends, place the magnet on the side of the blender near the cereal. Your child will notice the black fuzz collecting around the magnet's surface. This experiment works best the longer it sits.

Connecting Science with Fiction:

Poppy's story provides a wonderful opportunity for parents and children to discuss the things that bug them. Create a Venn diagram (see Scientist's Notebook, p. 132) to see what you and your child have in common. This is one way to open the lines of communication and improve your relationship.

Build a monster story: Have your child draw monsters, making sure he emphasizes the creature's physical characteristics. Then, have him create a habitat for his monster: A house, a cereal box, the woods, etc. Next, develop a problem the monster can solve and come up with a way to solve it. Wrap everything with a happy ending or a not-so-happy ending. Have your child take all these steps and combine into a monster book.

TAKE IT FURTHER:

- Repeat this experiment using cereals with lesser amounts of elemental iron. Have your child compare the amounts of iron he is able to remove from each type of cereal.
- For a messy follow-up, allow your child to open the Ziploc bag and drag the magnet through the water and cereal slurry. It will be gross, but he will be able to remove more iron pieces. Rinse off the magnet and dry well after each attempt.
- Let the bag burp! If you allow the water and cereal slurry to sit in the bag for a week, it will begin to ferment. As it ferments, carbon dioxide gas will build up inside the bag, and the bag will expand. This one is so gross, it's fun!

SCIENTIST'S NOTEBOOK FOR *A MONSTER IN MY CEREAL*

Venn Diagram:

What Do You Have in Common???

Use this Venn diagram to see what you have in common with your mom and dad so you can avoid misunderstandings like Poppy's. Put things you have in common in the center where the circles intersect. Feel free to copy this sheet and make separate charts for other parents and siblings and in your family!

Parent   Child

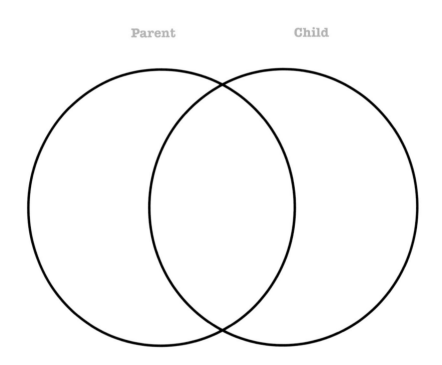

PART III

Air Science and Engineering

NOTES:

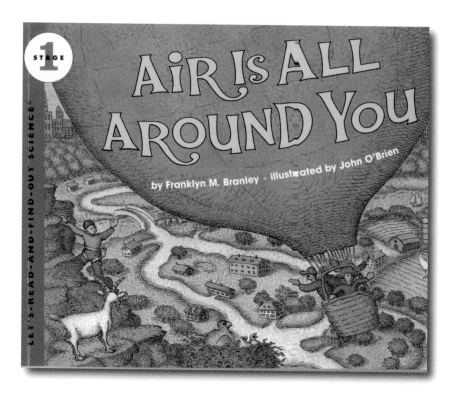

CHAPTER 15
Air Is All Around You

By Franklyn M. Branley.
John O'Brien, illustrator.
HarperCollins, New York: 1986/2006.

Another good read: *Feel the Wind* by Arthur Dorros.

THE STORY:

Air may be invisible, but this charming illustrated book gives kids a fun "look" at the stuff that enables human life. As the title suggests, air is everywhere: In our houses and yards, inside our bodies, cups and glasses, and even in water, though we can't breathe that air. Colorful drawings help to depict how, for example, air surrounds planet Earth like an orange peel, or that a room full of the seemingly weightless stuff would actually weigh as much as an average 5th grader if you put it on a scale!

The book will get your child thinking about the natural substance he probably most takes for granted. The simple tests will give definitive proof that the stuff exists! Then he will be ready for some fun with balloons and hot air.

• •

THE SCIENCE:

Inflate a balloon with hot air & a soda bottle!

The air we breathe is not pure oxygen but a mixture made mostly of nitrogen (roughly 78 percent), oxygen (about 21 percent), and trace amounts of gases including argon (about 1 percent), carbon dioxide (.03 percent), hydrogen, helium, methane, and water vapor. Together they combine to make up a "gas cocktail" full of tiny molecules.

In the experiment, your child will make those molecules move and actually inflate a balloon. First, he'll attach a balloon to an empty soda bottle which, as he should now understand, is filled with air. The balloon will trap the air molecules inside the glass bottle. When you and your child heat the bottle by immersing it in hot water, the air molecules will begin to move quickly and expand outward. This will cause the air to expand and rise upward into the balloon, and - presto! - the balloon inflates.

When you remove the bottle from the hot water and place it in a bath of cold water, the air molecules will start to cool and move more slowly. As they contract, the air molecules will sink toward the bottom of the bottle, causing the balloon to deflate.

HOT AIR RISING:

You don't have to be a scientist to know that hot air rises because it is lighter and less dense than cool air. The cooler the air inside the bottle, the denser and heavier it becomes, so it sinks and takes up less space. Try this next time you bring home a Mylar balloon: Leave it in a hot environment, like your car in summertime, and bring it into a cold room no more than 2 hours later (or let's say 30 minutes if your summers are really hot!). The balloon will appear to be less inflated because the air has contracted.

Can you feel the air?

This experiment is quick and simple. Your job will be to make your child "see" the air and understand what is happening to this "invisible" substance. You can help him understand by asking or suggesting the following (with **hints** for parents):

Try to "create" air that you can feel or see.

(**Hint:** blow it or move it or fan it.)

Now put your hand in front of your face and breathe. Can you feel anything?

(**Hint:** It's Air!) What happens when you wave your arms up and down a few times? Do you feel anything?

Explore the house, and try to find objects or creatures that can make air move. Can you list a few household items or tasks that move air? (Hint: Overhead fans, wind through the windows, opening the freezer door, closing a door quickly, the family dog, and so forth.)

Demonstrate that there is air inside the bottle. If you blow air over the bottle's opening, the air inside will vibrate and produce a whistling sound. Blow into the bottle and make the sound. Let your child try.

TALKING IT OVER:

Before you start, have your child observe an empty glass soda bottle and ask: What does it look like? How big is it? What shape? Do you see anything inside the bottle?

 (**Hint:** Remember that something could be in the bottle, even if it's invisible.)

As you go, ask your child questions at each step and give him time to think about the answers. Have him write his answers if you like.

How do you think a glass bottle could blow up a balloon using only the air that is already inside? Remember, you cannot cut the bottle, fill it with another substance, or remove the balloon.

What do you think will happen to the balloon when we put the bottle in the hot water container? What about in cold water?

Did the balloon do what you thought? What do you think happened to it?

THE EXPERIMENT & what you'll need:

- 3 plastic shoe/storage boxes
- Tap water (fill the box half way with water)
- 2 cups ice
- Tea kettle or pot containing water
- 1 glass soda bottle
- 8-inch balloon
- Thermometer

 1. Put the water on to boil in the tea kettle.

2. Place a balloon on the mouth of the glass soda bottle. This step will require some teamwork since little hands might not be able to position the balloon properly. One person should attach the balloon while the other holds the bottle. Note that scientists typically work in teams!

3. Fill a shoebox halfway with ice cubes and pour in the cold water. Now touch the box. Is it cold? Use the thermometer to take a temperature reading and note the result on the Data Sheet.

4. Fill the second shoebox halfway with hot water from the tap (not boiling water). Feel the outside of the box and take a temperature reading of the water and write it down.

5. Fill the third shoebox halfway with tap water that is room temperature. This is the "control" box, and it will be subjected to changes of temperature, so you can check what happens and compare with the hot and cold boxes.

6. Place the bottle in the control box and see if the balloon changes in shape or size.

7. Put the bottle in the box of hot water. Pour some of the hot water over the side and the top of the bottle. What happens to the balloon?

    Hint: It should inflate!

8. Now remove the bottle and balloon from the hot water box and put it in the box of ice-cold water. Observe.

    Hint: The balloon should flatten out.

9. Repeat steps 2-8 several times.

TAKE IT FURTHER:

- If your child is interested in learning how air affects our weather, check out National Geographic's JASON Project at www.jason.org. Register your child for Operation: Monster Storms. The site features videos, hands-on experiments, and weather-related games.
- You can explore the science behind hot air rising and cool air sinking in the next chapter, *Hot-Air Henry*. Stay tuned!

AIR IS ALL AROUND YOU DATA SHEET

Note: *it is best to repeat this experiment several times to stress how the temperature of the water affects the air!*

TRIAL #1

Type of water	How does the plastic box feel?	Temperature of the water	Description of the balloon
Tap water			
Tap water + 2 cups of ice			
Hot water			

TRIAL #2

Type of water	How does the plastic box feel?	Temperature of the water	Description of the balloon
Tap water			
Tap water + 2 cups of ice			
Hot water			

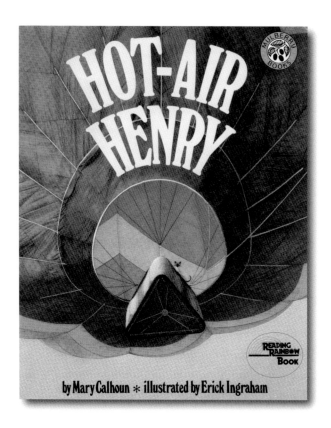

C H A P T E R   1 6
Hot-Air Henry

By Mary Calhoun.
Erik Ingraham, illustrator.
HarperCollins, New York: 1981.

Other good reads: *Hot Air: The (Mostly) True Story of the First Hot-Air Balloon Ride* by Marjorie Priceman; *The Mystery of the Hot-Air Balloon* by Gertrude Chandler Warner; *A Rainbow Balloon* by Ann Lenssen

THE STORY:

Your child will get a bird's-eye view of more than snowy landscapes when she reads about Henry, a Siamese cat who stows away on a hot-air balloon. Alone in the basket, Henry learns through trial and error how to control the balloon. He claws one cord to fire the burner and the balloon rises too high. Uh-oh! So then he swipes at another cord, the rip cord, which opens a hole at the top of the balloon to let out the hot air. The balloon sinks down again. Along the way, he chases blackbirds, roars at an eagle and tussles with a honking goose.

Your child can become a junior engineer and recreate Henry's adventure on a small scale by building a small-scale hot-air balloon made from a plastic bag.

THE SCIENCE:

Build Your Own Hot-Air Balloon!

Air, you may remember, is made up of molecules that are constantly in motion. As those air molecules warm up, they start to vibrate and bump into each other. This causes the space around each air molecule to grow bigger. Because each molecule uses more space for motion, the air expands and becomes less dense and therefore lighter weight. In other words, the same number of air molecules occupies a larger space.

We see the opposite effect when the air cools. As the temperature decreases, the molecules move more slowly. As they slow down, they take up less room. The amount of space the air takes up shrinks.

The science behind hot-air balloons is the same as the science behind the balloons you inflated or deflated in the previous chapter (*Air Is All Around You*) by heating or cooling the air inside the bottle.

A hot-air balloon has three essential parts: The burner, the balloon envelope, and the basket. The burner is a fuel jet that heats the air using propane gas — the same stuff we use to fire outdoor grills. The "balloon envelope" is the part that looks like a balloon. It traps the air and is the largest part of the apparatus. The basket, where passengers ride, is usually made of wicker since it is lightweight and flexible.

As the burner heats the air, the hotter air rises to the top of the balloon and cooler air sinks toward the bottom. Buoyancy — or the upward force of air on lighter-weight air - keeps this cooler air from escaping. Also, the process of convection keeps the cooler air dropping toward the burner as the hotter air rises (since it is less dense) to the top of the balloon. The burner is able to reheat the air, thus forcing the air back up into the envelope. If you have watched hot-air balloons, this is happening when the pilot "fires" the burner and the balloon envelope glows.

In this experiment a vegetable/fruit bag or a dry cleaning bag will act as your balloon envelope. Your hair dryer will act as the burner. Your child will place the bag over the top of the hair dryer so it can capture the hot air and force the cooler air in the bag to sink. The bag will become a mass of low-density air that floats upward in the higher, denser, cooler air surrounding it.

Connecting science with fiction:

Get your child thinking about his role as a junior engineer by asking him a few questions about flying.

Why do you think Henry wanted to fly?
Do you think he'd try it again?
Can you remember a time when you went flying?
What was that like?
What did it feel like?
Why do you think people enjoy flying?
Can you draw different ways that people can fly?

THE EXPERIMENT & what you'll need:

- Plastic vegetable/fruit bag or dry cleaning bag (let your child choose which kind, or try using both!)
- Drinking straws
- Handful of paper clips
- 2 wooden dowels, $\frac{5}{16}$ diameter
- String
- Scotch Tape
- Hair dryer

1. Draw a model of a hot-air balloon based on the description above. You can also find good pictures at Google Images (www.google.com/images) or How Stuff Works (http://science. howstuffworks.com).

2. Seal any openings and tears in the upper end of the bag with a minimum amount of tape. Too much tape will weigh down your balloon, and you will not get lift.

3. Roll the plastic around the lower opening upward as if you were rolling up pantyhose. Use one or two small pieces of tape to keep the roll in place.

4. Attach several paper clips to the plastic around the lower opening or tape straws along the fold. Remember: Either of these objects will add weight, and it is only through experimentation that you will figure out which one allows for greater lift.

Note: It is best to do the following steps outside or in a room with high ceilings.

5. **Mom or Dad:** Turn on the blow dryer on high, pointing up in the air, and have your child stretch the bag opening wide to capture the rising hot air. You might need another helper to support the upper end of the bag.

6. When the bag is completely inflated with hot air, let go of the balloon. If it rises quickly, stand back and let it fly. If it does not rise, continue heating it.

7.   If the bag tips over and spills the hot air before it reaches liftoff, add additional paper clips or straws to weigh down the bottom slightly. If the bag will not rise at all, remove a few clips, straws, or pieces of tape.

TAKE IT FURTHER:

- If your child gets hooked on "flying," try using different materials for balloon envelopes. Try tissue paper, large plastic garbage bags, or painter's thin plastic sheeting.
- Try to design a balloon with a larger surface area on top and a narrower, bottom opening. Use a wire coat hanger or wooden dowels to keep the bottom open.
- Research the nylon gore panel design used to create the modern balloon envelopes.
- Have your child create a blueprint for the new design.
- Have him test his new design and compare the results. Allow him time to "tweak" his design and re-test. This is the true work of engineers.
- Using your child's balloon as the setting, have him create an all-new adventure for *Hot-Air Henry*. Have your child research a location's topography and have him incorporate his research into his illustrations and story line.
- NASA has a wealth of information on hot-air balloons and on the science of flight. One section that might interest your child is NASA's Open Video Project. This free site allows you to access thousands of NASA videos. Just search "hot-air balloons" to learn more about these machines at http://open-video.org/
- You can also check out the one-minute video about the basics of hot-air ballooning at http://www.howstuffworks.com/hot-air-balloon.htm#. Click on the film icon on the right side of the page.

A note on decorating the balloons:

After your child has successfully launched her balloon, she may want to decorate it, since so often the hot-air balloons we see are colorful. However, paint and marker will weigh the bag down so it will not float. She may try, however, and see if there is any amount of decoration that is possible, then note the results and compare with the blank bag. This exercise will demonstrate how different variables can affect results.

She may also be interested to know that she's not the first scientist whose project has been grounded because of paint. In the early days of the Space Shuttle program, the original external fuel tank was painted white to match the orbiter and booster rockets. The engineers quickly learned that the excessive weight of the white paint prevented the shuttle from having enough thrust for liftoff. The NASA facility in New Orleans, which makes the external fuel tank, went back to the drawing board, and designed all future external tanks without the paint. The orange coloring we now see is the uncolored foam insulation sprayed on the tank.

SCIENTIST'S NOTEBOOK FOR *HOT-AIR HENRY*

Design your blueprint for your hot-air balloon.

NOTES:

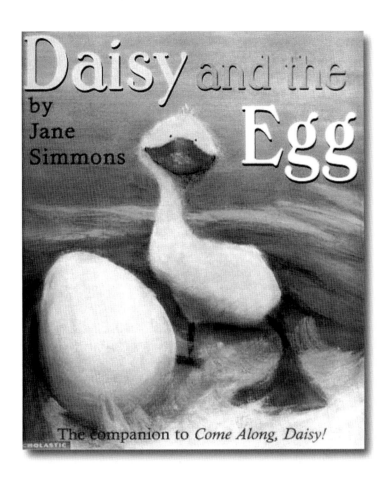

C H A P T E R   1 7
Daisy and the Egg

By Jane Simmons.
Hachette Children's Books, London, UK: 2003.

Another good read: *Horton Hatches the Egg* by Dr. Seuss

THE STORY:

In this charming picture book about patience, perseverance and determination, Daisy the duckling excitedly awaits the arrival of her baby brother. After her Aunt Buttercup's three eggs hatch and her cousins emerge, Daisy becomes impatient and asks if she can sit on her mama's green egg to help speed things up. But she is too little and can't stay on top. She finally decides to make a warm featherbed atop the egg and sits on top to keep it warm on a cold night. Daisy starts to fear the worst, but soon finds that her warm bed has protected the egg just as she had hoped.

Your child will take on Daisy's role as protector of an uncooked egg. His job will be to design a protective box that can cushion the egg when it is dropped (inside the box) from atop a ladder — much like an engineer would do. Along the way, he will learn about the durability of an egg's shell and its structure — not to mention patience, perseverance and determination in the face of a few broken eggs!

THE SCIENCE:

Design a "nest" to protect an egg in flight!

As you prepare to drop the egg in the egg box or boxes he builds, consider this: Eggshells are actually very strong when compressed. The curved shape of the eggshell allows force to be spread horizontally and vertically throughout the shell. You can think of this protective coating as being like the structural arch of a building. If stress is applied equally to the ends of the egg, it will not break. However, if an unbalanced force is applied to the sides of the egg, the outer, harder shell will give way first.

What this means for this experiment is that the best kind of protective box will cradle the egg evenly on all sides. Note that the thickness of an eggshell does not determine how strong it is. Thickness is just a measure of the chicken's nutrition, revealing how much calcium is deposited during the egg formation (inside the mother hen).

ANATOMY OF AN EGG

Each eggshell has three parts: Two internal membranes and an external shell. The internal membranes, known as the outer membrane and inner membrane, are flexible, porous, and rubbery. They give support to the fragile external shell. These membranes are made up of protein fibers that form a mesh-like structure to hold the albumen or egg white in place and provide a barrier against bacteria.

The external shell is made of a brittle, inflexible material called calcium carbonate, the same material that teeth are made of. One factor that determines the thickness of an eggshell is the amount of time it spends in the hen's uterus and the rate of calcium deposition during eggshell formation. The age of the hen also affects the thickness of the shell. As a hen ages, her "shell gland" will deposit less calcium around the inner membrane of the egg. Also, studies have found that eggshells are thinner during the hot summer months, since the blood chemistry of a hen changes slightly as her body is forced to breathe more quickly to stay cool.

Although the shell appears to be a solid structure, there are small pores in the outer shell that allow water vapor and air to transfer into and out of the egg. This helps the baby chick — which is called the embryo when it's inside the egg — to grow. What it means is that, while the external shell can be cracked, the internal shell will continue to hold the eggshell together. Check it out after your child cracks the eggs in this experiment. The soft internal shell will still hold on to the splintered pieces of the exterior shell.

Eggshells and architecture:

Arches, even those made of eggshells, are strong because they exert horizontal as well as vertical forces to resist the pressure of heavy loads. The crown of an eggshell can support heavy books or even the weight of a small child because the weight is distributed evenly along the structure of the egg. You can see this science used in architecture. Arches were originally used by the Romans around 300 B.C. They discovered that a semi-circular design provided superstrength in the construction of aqueducts and bridges. During the Medieval period in Europe, architects used arches to support the massive weight of cathedrals, castles, and governmental buildings. Today we see arches used mostly in the design of bridges, roadways, and in many football stadiums.

A note on materials for this experiment: In the spirit of engineering and ingenuity, your child needs to determine which materials to use in building his egg boxes. As a result, we will provide ideas but not definite amounts. Your child should come up with a hypothesis, design a "blueprint," construct his prototype, and then test it to see what happens. If the egg breaks, he will start over and then retest. I have found that this kind of experimentation with an unspecific materials list allows for wonderful designs.

THE EXPERIMENT & what you'll need:

- One dozen uncooked eggs (**Note:** If you don't want to use raw eggs, you can use hard-boiled eggs instead.)
- Ladder or stairwell
- Lightweight plastic fruit boxes (like strawberry, blueberry, or cherry tomato)
- Tape
- Digital camera (optional)

Possible materials to "pad" the egg box include but are not limited to: Newspaper, Styrofoam packing peanuts, foam rubber, including foam you can buy at craft stores, spray foam used in insulation, paper cups, balloons, paper towels, used panty hose, various recyclable materials around your home.

1. Kick off the challenge. "If Daisy's egg was dropped from the top of our house, stairwell, this stepstool, etc, how could she protect it?" Choose the location from which you will drop the egg — upstairs window, stairwell or ladder.

2. Build a box! If you were Daisy, what kind of box would you build to protect your baby brother's egg from breaking?

3. Work together to draw up plans that specify what materials you'll use and how each will protect the egg. You may choose to draw several different models. What other materials might you incorporate?

4. Do a practice run. Test the boxes in the kitchen or work area before the actual egg drop by dropping the egg box from the top of a chair or cabinet. Have extra eggs on hand for accidental breakage. And of course, if the egg breaks on the first test, change course! Figure out what didn't work and try to fix it.

5. Now you're ready for the real thing. Take the best boxes to your chosen location for the big egg drop.

6. Drop the egg box from the designated spot. Make sure to remove any fancy rugs or furniture! Let the box fall all the way to the floor.

7. Again, if the egg breaks, redesign the egg box based on the weakest point in the box. Repeat until you have successfully dropped the egg without breaking it.

153

TAKE SNAPSHOTS!

You can compare your results by drawing or taking digital pictures of the best boxes. You might take before and after pictures of each box and compare those. Can you explain which materials worked best? Why do you think those were the most effective materials?

TAKE IT FURTHER:

Try testing the successful egg box from a higher place to see if it is still successful at protecting the egg.

Check out how eggs get their shape at the Vermont 4-H's Virtual Farm website: http://www.ext.vt.edu/resources/4h/virtualfarm/poultry/poultry_incubation.html

• •

SCIENTIST'S NOTEBOOK FOR *DAISY AND THE EGG*

Use this page to design your box and brainstorm materials for the best egg cushion. circle the best ingredients and design!

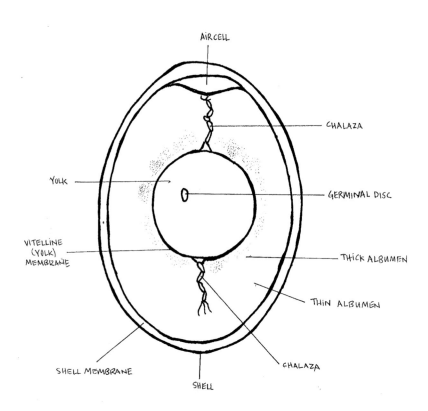

PART IV

Meteorology

NOTES:

By Barbara Shaw McKinney
Illustrated by Michael S. Maydak

CHAPTER 18
A Drop Around the World

By Barbara S. McKinney.
Michael S. Maydak, illustrator.
Dawn Publications, CA: 1998.

3

THE STORY:

With this illustrated poem about the water cycle, your child can accompany Drop, a droopy-faced, tear-shaped fellow, through the water cycle and view the world through his eyes as a liquid, gas, and solid. Your child can travel with Drop from a cloud in Maine to a steamy African jungle, where he transforms from mist to rainbow and finally fog. Along the way, you and your child can learn about our planet's water and its constant cycling.

After reading the book, you will construct a working model of the water cycle that will demonstrate in your own kitchen how water moves from one part of the cycle to another, morphing from steamy mist to cold clouds to rain and back again.

- -

THE SCIENCE:

Create a mini-water cycle in a jar!

Water is the source of all life on our planet, and we need water to survive. But have you ever really thought about where water comes from and why we never seem to run out?

As you see in Drop's saga, the Earth's water is constantly moving from above to below, to the surface of the Earth through the hydrologic cycle or water cycle. This cycle has no true beginning or ending place. It continuously converts water from a liquid to a gas then to a solid and back again — and has done so for the last million years. As long as we have heat from the sun, this incredible cycle will continue.

HERE IS HOW IT WORKS:

The cycle is controlled by the sun, which produces energy in the form of heat. This heat energy causes the water in the world's oceans, lakes, streams, and even puddles to warm up and evaporate. When water evaporates, it does not simply disappear. It actually changes from a liquid to a gas. This gas is called water vapor. Water evaporates from more than just bodies of water. It also evaporates from plants and wet soil in a process called "transpiration."

When water evaporates, it rises into the atmosphere since in its vaporized form, it is less dense than liquid water. The atmosphere contains cooler air. There, the water vapor molecules cool down and change back into liquid water. This is called condensation. For more information about condensation and how clouds form, see the chapter on *Sector 7*, p. 165.

As more and more water vapor cools into the clouds, the water droplets that form the clouds become larger and larger. These droplets get so big that the swirling winds in the atmosphere can no longer hold them up. The droplets fall from the sky in the form of rain, snow, sleet or hail, depending on the conditions in the atmosphere. These falling, condensed water molecules are known as precipitation.

Once the precipitation lands in a water source — meaning any body of water, from a puddle to an ocean, and even soil! — the cycle starts all over again. Fortunately for the Earth, this cycle never stops!

In this experiment, you'll put boiling water in a jar and watch it evaporate and turn into water vapor. As the water vapor rises in the jar, it meets with the cold surface of a pan. This cold surface causes the water vapor to condense and turn back into liquid water. The liquid water, in form of drops, hangs onto the surface of the pan until the drops become too large and heavy. When they become too large and heavy, they fall to the bottom of the jar as rain or precipitation.

THE EXPERIMENT & what you'll need:

- Boiling water
- Thick glass-canning jar
- Small aluminum pie pan or jar lid
- Ice cubes (preferably crushed)
- Flashlight

A NOTE REGARDING SAFETY:

This experiment uses boiling water and glass. An adult must be present to boil water and assist with this experiment.

BEFORE YOU BEGIN:

Ask your child: "Why doesn't the Earth ever run out of water?" Explain that he will construct a working model of the water cycle so that he can see how water moves from one part of the cycle to another.

1. Boil several cups of water to a temperature of 180 to 200 degrees Fahrenheit. Allow the boiling water to stop "bubbling" before pouring into the glass jar. Cold glass will crack if you change the temperature quickly.

2. While you wait, fill the jar lid or pie pan with crushed ice.

3. Place the lid or pie pan in the freezer for 5 minutes.

4. Fill ⅓ of the glass jar with boiling water. Be careful: A weak jar might crack at this temperature.

5. Place the pie pan or frozen, ice-filled lid over the jar's mouth. If you use the lid, place it atop the jar upside down. Do not screw it on or dump the ice into the hot water.

6. Darken the room and shine a flashlight through the backside of the jar.

7. Observe the water vapor traveling to the top of the jar from the surface.

8. After 4 minutes, lift up the pan or lid and observe the "raindrops" that are forming on the bottom of the pan.

9. Replace the pan or lid onto the top of the jar. Wait for 10 minutes until "raindrops" begin to fall from the bottom of the pan into the hot water.

10. As the "rain" falls, you may notice a swirling cloud forming inside the jar. This is a convection current transferring heat energy. That means you are seeing less dense hot air rising as the cooler and denser air sinks toward the water's surface. Convection currents are one cause of wind on our planet.

Why conserve water?

Although it's true that the water cycle never stops, it is still important to conserve water when you can. More than three-fourths of the Earth's surface is covered by water. This water is constantly being recycled through the water cycle. However, most of the Earth's water is not suitable for us to consume because it consists of salt water. That means that only 1 percent of the Earth's fresh water is drinkable! Therefore, every human and animal on the planet must share this precious resource and protect it from overuse and pollution.

Conserving water protects it and helps the Earth's environment. It protects drinking water supplies. Conserving also protects the habitats of freshwater marine creatures whose habitats and water sources are polluted. By conserving, you ease the burden on wastewater, or sewage, treatment plants. The less water we use, the less work these plants have to do to make water clean again.

Your family can save energy and money by conserving water. The local water supplier must use energy to treat and move water to your home. Your family uses energy to heat water for showers, laundry, and cooking. The less water your family and water supplier use, the lower the electric or gas bill!

CONNECTING SCIENCE WITH FICTION:

Watching your own personal "Drop" go through the water cycle, illustrate his passage from boiling water to condensed droplet to "rain." Give your drop a name and tell his story. Does he like living in a jar? Does he have friends there? Maybe a special friend?

TAKE IT FURTHER:

* Figure out your family's water consumption. Keep track of how much water each family member uses in a day by calculating how much time each person leaves the sink running, how long the shower is on, the number of times each person flushes the toilet, and how long the garden hose or sprinkler system is used. Create a bar graph of each person's usage, and have a family meeting to come up with ways to conserve more water.

* In order to reinforce the concept of the water cycle, have your child read *The Many Adventures of Drippy the Raindrop*. This online book, which will also read the story to your child, follows Drippy through all stages of the hydrologic cycle. http://www.kimballmedia.com/Drippy/DrippysWorldTrialStories/ToMountainsAndBack/Entry.htm.

* Put on a play! The Incredible Water Show by Debra Frasier (available on Amazon.com) contains a script for a play about the water cycle. You can round up your kids and some friends and set up a stage in the backyard.

* If your kid is addicted to video games, have him try an educational adventure game from NASA called "Droplet and the Water Cycle." Help Droplet find his way back home to the atmosphere after he lands in a rainforest, but watch out! Danger lurks around every corner! To access this free game go to http://kids.earth.nasa.gov/droplet.html.

162

SCIENTIST'S NOTEBOOK FOR A DROP AROUND THE WORLD

Use this space for notes or to illustrate the adventure of your own personal "Drop" created in the jar.

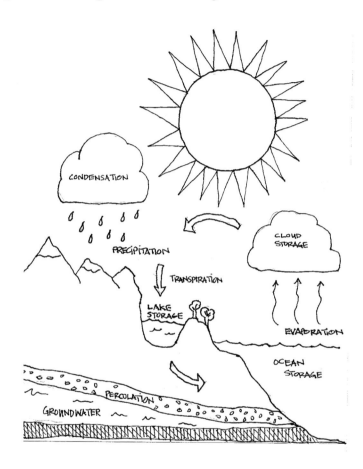

NOTES:

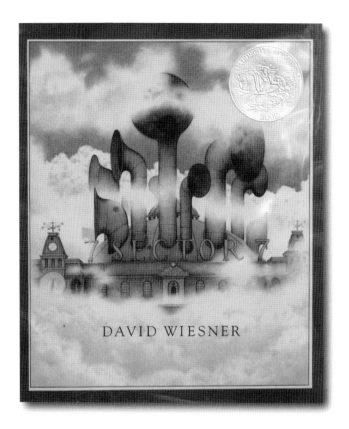

CHAPTER 19
Sector 7

By David Wiesner.
Houghton Mifflin Harcourt, New York: 1999.

Other good reads: *The Cloud Book* by Tomie de Paola;
Cloud Dance by Thomas Locker; *The Man Who Named the
Clouds* by Julie Hannah and Joan Holub

THE STORY:

If your kids have ever asked you where clouds come from, then this pictures-only book will give them something to daydream about. The story unfolds image-by-image, as a friendly, smiling cloud whisks a schoolboy away from a field trip to the Empire State building in New York. They fly over skyscrapers to "Sector 7," a floating "cloud dispatch center" that determines cloud shapes and sizes and resembles Grand Central Station.

When he hears complaints from the clouds that they are bored with their own shapes, the young boy starts drawing blueprints for fantastical new cloud designs. But that infuriates Sector 7's bureaucrats, who send the boy back to his schoolmates by way of a cloud taxi. Still, back at Sector 7, the clouds refuse to back down after catching a glimpse of imaginative free will. The sky fills with misty, floating sea creatures.

This beautifully illustrated, imaginative tale is a great "jumping-off point" to discover how clouds form in a bottle — your own kitchen-counter "Sector 7"!

. . . .

THE SCIENCE:

Your very own ecosystem with clouds!

Clouds form from water that has evaporated from oceans, rivers, lakes, streams, and pools, or from wet soil and plants. Water evaporates when the sun's rays heat it up. Though it seems that the water has simply dried, it actually turns into water vapor, which is the gaseous state of water. Evaporated water, also called water vapor, expands and cools as it rises into the atmosphere.

The air in our atmosphere can hold only a certain amount of water vapor. Warm air can hold more water vapor than cool air can. When the temperature drops, some of the water vapor begins to condense — or change into a liquid by forming tiny water droplets. This is known as **condensation**. You see condensation all the time: A cool mirror in the bathroom after a hot, steamy shower, for example, or a glass of ice water "sweating" on a hot day.

WHY CLOUDS ARE WHITE

In order for water vapor to condense, it must condense around something very small, like a dust particle. These particles, called **condensation nuclei**, become the centers of the droplets. Many condensation nuclei are tiny salt particles, ash, dust particles, or smoke particles floating in the air.

Note that without condensation nuclei, we would not be able to see clouds. The dust, ash, smoke, and salt give clouds their "white" coloring. Without it, clouds would basically be invisible to our eyes. Meanwhile, the droplets that settle on the nuclei are tiny; most measure between $\frac{1}{2,500}$ and $\frac{1}{250}$ inch (0.01 to 0.1 millimeter) in diameter — that is smaller than the width of a pin head!

MAKING A CLOUD

In this experiment your child will witness how clouds form by using a capped plastic bottle as the "atmosphere" and tap water as the body of water that will form vapors. The first part of the experiment demonstrates cloud formation using cold water and a match. After closing the bottle with the match inside, you will see a small cloud-like structure over the cold water. This forms when smoke particles from the match cling to the small amount of water vapor in the bottle.

The second part of the experiment uses hot water. You'll notice that the cloud becomes much larger and more visible. That is because hot water evaporates more quickly into water vapor. The water vapor will mix with the smoke particles. Those particles in turn provide a cool surface on which the water molecules can condense. Meanwhile, when you squeeze the bottle, that movement mimics the convection current in our atmosphere that pushes warm air up and cold air down. So it's a mini weather system that creates the "seeds" for a larger and more visible cloud.

Let it snow!

Snow starts just like a cloud, only at a lower temperature. If the temperature is cold enough in the upper atmosphere, water vapor does not condense and form liquid droplets. Instead, the water vapor turns directly to ice through a process called **sublimation**. For sublimation to occur, the temperature must be at or above -40 degrees Fahrenheit (-40 degrees Celsius). Small particles similar to condensation nuclei must also be present in the atmosphere. These particles are known as freezing nuclei. They can be made of dust particles, salt pieces, or smoke particles.

THE EXPERIMENT & what you'll need:

- 2 identical clear two-liter plastic bottles with caps
- ⅓ cup cold tap water
- ⅓ cup hot tap water (100 degrees)
- Measuring cup
- Funnel
- Matches

Safety warning: This experiment uses lighted matches. An adult must be present to do this portion of the experiment.

Part I

1. Place a funnel into the mouth of a two-liter water bottle.

2. Pour ⅓ cup of cold water into the two-liter bottle and cap the bottle.

3. Shake the bottle for 30 seconds and set it on the table.

4. Squeeze and un-squeeze the bottle several times with the cap on it. Look inside the bottle. Do you see anything different from before?

5. Remove the cap on the bottle.

6. Light a match and allow it to burn for two seconds.

7. Hold the lighted match over the mouth of the bottle, then quickly blow it out.

8. Drop the smoking matchstick into the bottle. Make sure the smoke of the match gets into the bottle and quickly cap it.

9. Squeeze and release the bottle five times. Now do you see any changes?

    A cloud should form at the top of the bottle.

Part II

10. Place a funnel into the mouth of the second two-liter bottle. Pour in ⅓ cup of hot water.

11. Repeat steps 3-9.

TALKING IT OVER:

As your child goes through both parts of the experiment, ask her continually to observe what's going on inside the bottle. Questions to help guide you both through the experiment:

What happens when you squeeze the bottle?

What happens after you release the squeeze?

Why is the cloud larger this time with the hot water?

Note: Squeezing the bottle forces the particles and water droplets to compress quickly and move upward in the bottle.

Releasing the bottle cools the air off. The invisible particles of smoke help the tiny droplets to stick together more easily. The result is a "puff" of tiny droplets — a.k.a. a cloud.

CONNECTING SCIENCE WITH FICTION:

Sector 7 is a wordless picture book. Have your child become the "author" and create the words to accompany David Wiesner's intricate illustrations. What is the boy's name? The friendly cloud?

Where would you go if a cloud whisked you away? Pose this question to your child and have her brainstorm the places and things she would see. Create a new cloud story to share with family and friends.

If you had been whisked to Sector 7, what cloud designs would you come up with? Draw your clouds!

TAKE IT FURTHER:

- Show your child how water droplets collect around condensation nuclei in this excellent animation by National Geographic's JASON Project. Go to www.Jason.org to register and log in first. Check out: http://www.jason.org/ and click on "Monster Storms" on the left-hand side of the screen. When the Monster Storms logo appears, click on "Videos & Animations." Once on the "Videos & Animations" page, scroll down to "Mission 2" and click on the "condensation" animation short.
- While visiting the JASON project, explore the resources found in Mission 2: The Plot Condenses Here you can find print materials and video clips on the water cycle and cloud formation, and in the digital lab section, you can even play a video game: "Understanding Clouds."
- To learn more about the cloud types and how they affect our weather, see Web Weather for Kids at http://www.eo. ucar.edu/webweather/cloud3.html. At this site your child can view the common cloud types seen over North America,

learn their atmospheric position and composition, and play digital cloud games.

- Go outside and watch the clouds. Have your child keep a picture journal of the cloud types she sees overhead. After about a week of keeping track of the clouds, she may begin to notice patterns about cloud types and the weather you are having. You might have a budding meteorologist on your hands!

SCIENTIST'S NOTEBOOK FOR SECTOR 7

Use this page to illustrate the clouds you created in your bottles and draw new blueprints for cloud designs in your own Sector 7 factory!

C H A P T E R   2 0
Twister!

By Darleen Bailey Beard.
Nancy Carpenter, illustrator.
Farrar, Straus and Giroux, New York: 1999.

Good reads: *Night of the Twister* by Ivy Ruckman
(older readers); *Tornados* by Gail Gibbons;
Tornadoes by Seymour Simon

THE STORY:

Could your child imagine living through a tornado? In this thrilling and colorful book, Natt and Lucille do just that. What begins as a lazy summer day of popsicle-eating and swinging on the porch becomes a frightening "gully washer" of a storm. Purple skies bring lightning and raindrops, and then their Mama yells, "Twister!" Safe in the storm cellar, Natt and Lucille listen to the wind and hail pounding at the cellar's roof. Later, they emerge to survey the damage.

Twister, with its detailed and realistic portrayal of life in "tornado alley," serves as a great introduction to this frightening and most dangerous weather phenomenon. After you've read it, you can build a "vortex in a bottle" to help your child understand how tornadoes are formed.

• •

THE SCIENCE:

Make a water tornado in a bottle!

Tornadoes are considered the most violent storms on earth and produce the fastest recorded wind speeds of any type of storm. Tornadoes can hit in every continent on earth but strike the most in North America, especially the United States. In an average year, more than 800 tornadoes will blow through the United States. But why and how do these major storms form?

A tornado is simply a violently rotating column of air extending from a thunderstorm to the ground. The most violent tornadoes are capable of tremendous destruction, with wind speeds of 250 mph (miles per hour) or greater. Damage paths can be in excess of a mile wide and 50 miles long.

Tornadoes are created within powerful thunderstorms called **super cells** or **mesocyclones**. These powerful storm clouds usually form at the point where a dry, cold air front moving to the east meets with a warm and wet air front. Within these cells, quickly moving areas called updrafts are supplying warm and humid air to the clouds. This warm and wet air acts as fuel, intensifying and strengthening the storm.

Under the right conditions, winds within the cloud can begin to spin in different directions. Within a super cell there is an area of strong rotation. As this spinning becomes faster and more concentrated, a narrow column of spinning air forms at the base of the super cell cloud. This phenomenon is called a **vortex**, and it is a low-pressure area surrounded by swirling winds. A vortex acts like a vacuum pulling the surrounding air into itself. The air is cooled and condensation takes place, triggering a process of convection currents in which warm air rises and colder air sinks to lower levels of the clouds. That, in turn, gives further velocity to the spinning air around the low-pressure center. If this spinning column of air drops from the cloud but does not touch the ground, it is called a funnel cloud. When a funnel cloud touches the ground, it becomes a tornado.

Air is usually invisible, so why can you see a tornado? There are two answers to this question. To start, condensation is occurring around the low pressure center known as the vortex. As the air cools, water vapor is changed from gas into liquid water, so you can see large collections of these drops. However this is not the main reason why you see a tornado. The swirling winds around the vortex pick up dust, dirt, and debris from the storm's path. The more dust and debris the storm picks up, the more visible it becomes. This debris is circulated through the spinning column of air and dropped back to the ground.

Sound effects

You can also hear a tornado. It sounds like a heavily loaded freight train coming toward you! You also might hear hailstones, like Natt and Lucille do in Twister. Hail forms because of the strong downdrafts forcing frozen drops of rain out of the tops of the cumulonimbus or thunderstorm clouds. Instead of these frozen drops being a part of the convection loop, basically traveling from the top to the bottom of the cloud and back again, they are sent spiraling downward at high speeds.

In this experiment, your child will construct a model of a vortex in a bottle. The model will demonstrate how debris — in this case, glitter, confetti or dried herbs — circulates around the vortex and is eventually dropped by the storm. You should make sure to recreate the model several times, using different-sized pieces of debris for comparison.

The vortex in this experiment is made of water and not air as in a real tornado. Your child may recognize this and refer to it as a whirlpool. That whirlpool is also known as a water vortex. Remember, a vortex is a mass of fluid or air that moves in a circular motion to form low pressure in its center. This low-pressure center acts like a vacuum, picking up the debris. A water vortex works with water much the same way a tornado works with air. A vacuum action tends to draw everything around a vortex toward its center.

You will also change the hole size of the washer when you repeat this experiment. This slight change will help you introduce the concept of **variables**, which are minor modifications that might affect the results of an experiment. The washer's hole size may affect the speed at which the water moves. Have your child observe this carefully, since the speed of the water is determined by how rapidly debris spins and moves through the vortex. This is where your repetition of the experiment will come in handy.

A TORNADO IS NOT A HURRICANE!

You really cannot compare tornadoes with hurricanes. The only thing these two storm types have in common is that they are both atmospheric vortices with an area of extreme low-pressure at their center. Hurricanes, as you probably know, are oceanic "events," meaning they start and then gather steam over the ocean. Tornadoes are terrestrial, or land-based, events. Hurricanes also will sometimes have tornadoes "embedded" in them, and they can provide ideal conditions for tornadoes to form.

But hurricanes are much larger in size and duration than tornadoes: they can be hundreds of kilometers wide in diameter, versus hundreds of meters wide like tornadoes. And they are also purely oceanic and will lose steam and wither soon after landfall (though not soon enough for some towns in their path!). In fact, it's shortly after a hurricane hits land that tornadoes can develop — on the right side of the hurricane's eye wall.

Once a tornado develops, it can travel up to 10 miles on the ground. Typically, tornadoes move along their path at 20 to 45 miles per hour. They do not remain on the ground the entire time, but often rise back into the cloud as they re-create themselves.

THE EXPERIMENT & what you'll need:

- 2 two-liter clear plastic soda bottles
- Scissors
- Duct tape
- Marking pen
- Enough water to fill the bottles
- Glitter, sparkles, Mylar confetti or any other small visible material that does not dissolve in water, such as oregano leaves or rosemary leaves
- 2 metal or rubber washers that have the same outside diameter as the mouth of the bottles, one with a small center hole and one with a larger center hole. (You can find washers at hardware stores such as Lowe's, Home Depot, and Ace, in the section with screws, nuts, and bolts. If you're unsure, bring your bottle to the hardware store to see if the washer fits on — not in — the mouth of the bottle.)

1. Label one bottle "A" and the other "B" with your marking pen.

2. Create your control by filling "Bottle A" about two-thirds full of tap water.

3. Sprinkle a pinch or two of the glitter, Mylar confetti or other visible material into "Bottle A."

4. Make sure "Bottle B" is empty. Place "Bottle B" upside down on top of "Bottle A. "

5. Make sure the mouths of the two bottles are aligned exactly to prevent leakage.

6. Tape the mouths of the two bottles tightly together with the duct tape. You can test for leakage by carefully tilting the bottles sideways. Be advised that there will be some minor leakage.

7. Turn the bottles over so that bottle A (with the water in it) is on top of bottle B.

8. Quickly swirl the bottles five to seven times, just like you would spin a hula-hoop. Make sure to grip the center of this model where the tape is located. You should also place your hand on top of the bottle holding water to support it.

9. Set the bottles down and watch the vortex spin, noting the shape and speed of the swirling water.

10. Repeat the above step, this time observing how many times a piece of "debris" spins around. Record the count on your data sheet. (**Note to parents:** You'll find that your children will make better observations if you do this part in two steps so that they can indulge their fascination the first time around, then time it the second!)

11. Untape the bottles and tape the washer with the larger hole to the mouth of "Bottle A." Do not cover the washer hole with tape. Repeat steps 2-10 and record the details on your data sheet.

12. Untape the bottles and tape the washer with the smaller hole to the mouth of "Bottle A." Do not cover the washer hole with tape. Repeat steps 2-10.

13. When you have all results on your data sheet, compare how the size of the washers' holes affects the shape and speed of the water vortex.

Connecting Science with Fiction

Darleen Bailey Beard uses highly descriptive language to express how the storm intensifies and the damage it leaves behind. At times the storm is even captivating and beautiful: "Hailstones sparkle like glittering diamonds." Have your child remember a storm he has experienced. Have him make drawings of the event or the aftermath. Then have him describe one aspect of the storm that was beautiful.

Have your child collect oral histories from different family members about their storm experiences, including tornadoes, hurricanes, floods, and snowstorms. Once he has the stories, either written down or as recorded audio files, go to the library or go online and find photographs of the storms to accompany your family's storm histories. Put the histories and photographs into a book, podcast (for the tech-savvy), or Power Point presentation to share.

TAKE IT FURTHER:

Explore your variables!

- Try using water at different temperatures to see if the change affects the shape of the vortex or speed of the water.
- Try out different "liquid debris" materials, like sugar water, syrup or soda to see how they affect the vortex.
- Change the bottles' sizes to determine if that affects your results.

- Learn more about tornadoes online:

  FEMA for Kids teaches tornado facts and gives tips on how to be safe during a tornado. Here, kids can learn about the Fujita scale for measuring tornado intensity, do tornado math, and find stories and games. Go to http://www.fema.gov/kids/tornado.htm

The National Weather Service's "Owlie and the Owl" story is a fun coloring book that teaches factual information and tornado preparedness in a non-frightening manner (which will teach kids not to panic when a storm strikes). To download and copy this book, go to: http://www.weather.gov/os/brochures/owlie-tornado.pdf

● ●

TWISTER DATA SHEET

How quickly does debris spin through the vortex?

Focus on one piece of debris within the bottle. Count the number of times it spins around and through the vortex. Record that information on the chart below. Then compare how the size of the hole affects the speed at which the debris moves.

Test Bottle	Speed of debris – how many turns?
Control bottle with no washer	Turns
Large washer	Turns
Small washer	Turns

Now, try drawing or coloring what the vortex looks like during each test of this experiment

Your Drawing			
			181

| Test Bottle | Control bottle | Large washer | Small washer |

ACKNOWLEDGEMENTS:

From the author

The idea for this book has been many years in the making. It all began back in 1999 when I went to work for Isidore Newman School as a Lower School science teacher. I was intrigued by the notion of blending scientific concepts with children's literature to promote both scientific inquiry and literacy in the classroom.

One afternoon in 2000, I was chatting with some fellow educators about my idea for an integrated science and literature curriculum during a professional conference in Atlanta. My colleagues loved the idea and encouraged me to pursue it. From that day on, I have been refining, questioning, and testing ideas out on my students as I developed the curriculum.

In 2001, I presented my idea to Kitty Greenberg, then assistant to the headmaster at Newman, and to Joan Starr, assistant headmistress. They recommended that I share ideas about my program and swap information with other Lower School teachers, both at Newman and at other area schools. By then, I had already started experimenting with the curriculum during labs. But Joan and Kitty's enthusiasm for my idea and faith in my abilities led me to forge ahead at full steam. Once the program was in full swing, I began to present it officially to other schools and at national educational and science conferences.

Thanks to my conference presentations and now this book, the information and source material has been checked, re-checked, and expanded. I must thank my librarian friends, Tiffany Stanley Abshire and Sandra Rivet, for their help in selecting literature to accompany the science experiments and for their support in developing this notion. I am indebted to Sandra Kellermann Cvitanovic for helping me prepare and organize the presentations.

Thanks must also go to my teacher friends at Isidore Newman School, and at the public schools in Plaquemines Parish (Martha Grisso), Jefferson Parish (Wendy Savelle), and Orleans Parish Public Schools for testing experiments and activities and then giving me honest feedback. I am indebted to Ann Wilson and Jean May-Brett of the Louisiana Department of Education and to Brenda Nixon of Louisiana State University for providing me with sources on the present state of science education in the United States and on integrating literature into science. And of course, I am very grateful to the Isidore Newman School administration for trusting me with the science and for giving me the freedom to develop a curriculum (and book!) that fits the needs and creativity of our students.

I must also acknowledge my new friends at Bright Sky Press for believing in this manuscript and for guiding me through this new and strange process. First, thank you to Nora McAlister, a Bright Sky owner and Newman parent, for stopping me one day in the hallway at school and asking me if I wanted to write a book. To Lucy Chambers for her gentle influence and her willingness to answer all of my questions. I am indebted to Nora Shire for her persistence with the publishing world and with getting permissions to use the books mentioned. I gratefully acknowledge Shelley Pannill Stein, who had to toil over the manuscript so that it would make as much sense to lay people as it does to "science nerds." Thank you for "tweaking" the manuscript.

And finally, I wish to thank the hundreds of kindergarten through fourth grade students who have walked into my lab for the past ten years and given me honest criticism about experiments that worked or did not work. Thank you so much for loving science and always wanting more. I do this for you.

PUBLISHER INFORMATION

By Chapter:

1. *Wizzil:* Jacket design from Wizzil by William Steig, pictures by Quentin Blake. Text copyright © 2000 by William Steig. Pictures copyright © 2000 by Quentin Blake. Reprinted by permission of Farrar, Straus and Giroux, LLC., NY. ISBN: 978-0-374-38466-1.

2. *Strega Nona:* Summary and book cover reprinted with the permission of Simon & Schuster Books for Young Readers, an imprint of Simon & Schuster Children's Publishing Division, NY, from Strega Nona by Tomie de Paola. Copyright © 1975, Tomie de Paola. ISBNs: 0-671-66283-X, hardback; 9780671662837.

3. *George's Marvelous Medicine:* Text by Roald Dahl and illustrations by Quentin Blake, copyright © 1981. Summary and book cover art used by permission of Penguin Group (USA) Inc., Books for Young Readers, NY. ISBNs: 08085959199; 9780142410356.

4. *Bartholomew and the Oobleck:* "Book Cover," copyright ©1949, renewed 1976, from Bartholomew and the Oobleck written and illustrated by Dr. Seuss. Used by permission of Random House Children's Books, a division of Random House, Inc., NY. ISBNs: 0394800753; 9780394800752.

5. *The Book of Slime:* Text copyright © 1997 by Ellen Jackson. Illustration copyright © 1997 by Jan Davey Ellis. Millbrook Press, CN. Summary and book cover art used with permission of the author and the illustrator. ISBN: 9780761300945.

6. *The Butter Battle Book:* "Book Cover," copyright © 1984, from The Butter Battle Book written and illustrated by Dr. Seuss. Used by permission of Random House Children's Books, a division of Random House, Inc. ISBN: 9780394965802

7. *Chocolate Fever:* Written by Robert Kimmel Smith with illustrations by Gioia Fiammenghi. Copyright © 2006. Summary and book cover art used by permission of the publisher, Penguin Group (USA), Inc., Books for Young Readers, NY. ISBNs: 0142405957; 9780142405956.

8. *Ice Cream Larry*: Written by Daniel Manus Pinkwater, copyright© 1999, and illustrations by Jill Pinkwater, copyright © 1999. Summary and book cover art used by permission of Marshall Cavendish Children's Books, Tarrytown, NY. ISBNs: 9780761451860; 0-761451862 (pbk).

9. *Sad Sam and the Magic Cookies*: Written by Stacy Quest, copyright © 2007, and illustrations by Michael Morris, copyright © 2007, is available through BookBound Publishing, Los Angeles. www.bookboundpublishing.com Permission to use the summary and the book cover art given by the publisher. ISBN: 978-1932367010.

10. *Everybody Bakes Bread* by Norah Dooley and illustrated by Peter J. Thornton. Copyright © 1996 by Carolrhoda Books. Reprinted with the permission of Carolrhoda Books, a division of Lerner Publishing Group, Inc. All rights reserved. No part of this excerpt may be used or reproduced in any manner whatsoever without the prior written permission of Lerner Publishing Group, Inc., Minneapolis, MN. ISBN: 978-0876148952.

11. *How to Make an Apple Pie and See the World*: "Book Cover," copyright © 1994 by Marjorie Priceman, author and illustrator. Used by permission of Alfred A. Knopf, an imprint of Random House Children's Books, a division of Random House, Inc., NY. ISBNs: 0079880836; 9780679837053.

12. *Rechenka's Eggs*: Written and illustrated by Patricia Polacco, copyright © 1988. Summary and book cover art used by permission of the publisher, Penguin Group (USA) Inc., Books for Young Readers, NY. ISBN: 9780698113855.

13. *Oliver's Milk Shake*: Text copyright © 2001 by Vivian French. Illustration copyright © 2001 by Alison Bartlett. Summary and book cover art used by permission of Orchard, an imprint of Hodder Children's Books, London, UK. ISBN: 9780531303047.

14. *A Monster in My Cereal*: Written by Marie-Francine Hebert, copyright © 1990. Illustrations by Philippe Germain, copyright © 1990. Published by Second Story Press, Toronto, Canada. Summary and book cover art used by permission of the publisher. ISBNs: 0-688-04068-3 (pbk); 9780688005016.

15. *Air Is All Around You*: Text copyright © 1986 by Franklyn M. Branley. Illustration copyright © 2006 by John O'Brien. Summary and book cover art used by permission of HarperCollins Publishers, NY. ISBN: 978-0060594138, pbk; 9780060594152.

16. *Hot-Air Henry*: Text copyright © 1981 by Mary Calhoun and illustrations copyright © 1981 by Erick Ingraham. Published by Mulberry Books, an imprint of William Morrow & Co. Summary and book cover art used by permission of HarperCollins Publishers, NY. ISBNs: 0-688-04068-3; 9780688005023.

17. *Daisy and the Egg*: Text and illustration copyright © 2003 by Jane Simmons. Summary and book cover art used by permission of Hachette Children's Books, London, UK. ISBNs: 9780316738729; 0316797855.

18. *A Drop Around the World*: Text copyright © 1998 by Barbara S. McKinney; illustration copyright ©1998 by Michael S. Maydak. Published by Dawn Publications, Nevada City, CA. Summary and book cover art used by permission of the publisher. ISBNs: 978-1883220723 (pbk); 978-1883220716.

19. *SECTOR 7* cover by David Wiesner. Jacket illustration and text copyright © 1999 by David Wiesner. Reprinted by permission of Clarion Books, an imprint of Houghton Mifflin Harcourt Publishing Company, NY. All rights reserved. ISBN: 978-0395746561.

20. *Twister*: Jacket design from Twister! by Nancy Carpenter. Author, Darleen Bailey Beard. Text copyright © 1999 by Darleen Bailey Beard. Pictures copyright © 1999 by Nancy Carpenter. Reprinted by permission of Farrar, Straus and Giroux, LLC., NY. ISBN: 9780374480141.

AUTHOR'S RESEARCH NOTES & BIBLIOGRAPHY

(1)   According the Center on Educational Policy, 43 percent of elementary schools in the United States have cut down on time given to science instruction in order to focus more class time on math and English language arts instruction. 2nd In one San Francisco Bay Area study, 80 percent of K–5th grade multiple-subject teachers in charge of teaching science in their classrooms reported spending 60 minutes or less per week on science — down from 125 percent in 2000. And 16 percent of those teachers reported they spent no time at all on science instruction in their classrooms.(3)

(2)   In one of several examples, American students scored 17th out of 30 industrialized nations on the science portion of the 2006 Program for International Student Assessment (PISA).(5) [cut-The PISA is sponsored by the Organization for Economic Cooperation and Development (OECD), an intergovernmental agency of 30-member countries.] In this test, students are asked to analyze data and apply conceptual knowledge to develop solutions to scientific problems rather than to recall basic scientific information.   187

(3)   The integration of scientific inquiry and literacy has reciprocal benefits for a child as skills are forged together, since they complement and naturally support each other. In 1996 the National Research Council developed the National Science Education Standards, which provide a framework for science learning. These standards stress inquiry throughout a child's education. Allowing a child to participate in scientific inquiry will help him learn new concepts and vocabulary. At the same time he'll learn how to make observations, ask questions and frame responses scientifically, construct written and spoken explanations, and communicate his understanding of science to others. These skills are not strictly science skills: they literacy competencies that will benefit a child throughout his education.

(4)   Children's books, fictional or non-, also helps parents and teachers introduce scientific concepts in a familiar and non-threatening manner, say the authors of *Science through Children's Literature: An Integrated Approach.* That works well because "the child's interest is sustained and the story structure helps them to comprehend and draw relationships between the material world and their own personal world."

Bibliography

American Association for the Advancement of Science AAAS (1993) *Benchmarks for Scientific Literacy.* Oxford: Oxford University Press. Page 322

Before It's Too Late, The National Commission on Mathematics and Science for the 21st Century. United States Department of Education: Washington, D.C.

Butzow, C., Butzow, J., and Ben-Zvi, H.L. (2000) *Science through Children's Literature: An Integrated Approach.* Teacher Ideas Press, Portsmouth, NH

Douglas, R. et.al. (2006) Linking Science and Literacy in the K – 8 Classroom. NSTA Press, Arlington, VA

Fulp, Sherri L. (2002). Status of elementary school science teaching. Horizon Research Inc.; North Carolina.

Glod, M. *U.S. Teens Trail Peers Around World on Math-Science Test.* Washington Post December 5, 2007: Washington, D.C. Page A07

Helping children learn at home. (1997, March 27). *Pointers for Parents* (National Science and Technology Week Publication SP/96-8). Arlington, VA: National Science Foundation.

McMurrer, J. (2007). Choices, changes, and challenges: Curriculum and instruction in the NCLB era. Center on Education Policy: Washington, D.C.

National Research Council (NCR). 1996. *National Science Education Standards.* National Academy Press, Washington, D.C.

Yoo, S. *Children's Literature for Developing Good Readers and Writer in Kindergarten.* 1997. Education, Vol. 118.